CEREBRAL PALSY & ME

MY AUTOBIOGRAPHY

GAVIN CLIFTON

Joanna

All the best,

Copyright © 2023 by Gavin Clifton - The Disabled Writer

All rights reserved. No part of this book may be reproduced or used in any manner without the prior written permission of the copyright owner, except for the use of brief quotations in a book review.

No portion of this book may be reproduced in any form without written permission from the publisher or author, except as permitted by UK copyright law. This book does not replace the advice of a medical professional.
To maintain the anonymity of the individuals involved, I have changed some details.
These are my memories, from my perspective, and I have tried to represent events as faithfully as possible.

Hardback ISBN: 979-8-8614-1544-6
Paperback ISBN: 979-8-8614-2229-1

Cover Photograph Copyright © 2023 by Clare Thomas
Book Design by Clare Thomas

Author Gavin Clifton
www.gavincliftonwriter.com
The Disabled Writer

ACKNOWLEDGMENTS

I want to express my heartfelt love and gratitude to all my family and friends for their fantastic support throughout my cerebral palsy journey. Your love, patience, encouragement, and understanding have been instrumental in helping me navigate the challenges and embrace the triumphs. I am truly blessed to have such an incredible support system by my side, and I can't thank you all enough for being there every step of the way.

I want to thank from the bottom of my heart Claire Tippings (my nursery years in primary and junior school) and all the nursery nurses after that, including Sandra Matthews, who is no longer with us, for their unconditional dedication and exceptional support that shaped my early years and has made me the strong, stubborn, and determined person I am now. Your guidance, care, and patience created a safe learning environment that allowed me to concentrate fully on my education and develop as a child and teenager. You will always have a special place in my heart.

I would like to thank my football coaches and supporting team, the likes of Robin Churchill, Steve Evans, Clive Huish, Howell Jones, and Tudor James, for, from the very start, including me in every training session, matchday squads, six-a-side tournament, and football tours and for ensuring my welfare and physical safety were prioritised. Even though I wanted to be involved all the time in my head, I know now I could not play more than my body allowed, and also because of the real chance that I could get hurt more quickly and more regularly than the rest of the players.

I want to express my sincere gratitude to my remarkable former work colleagues. Your friendship and unwavering support meant the world to me during our time together. I still cherish the bonds we forged, which continue to endure and bring joy to my life. Regardless of the challenges posed by my disability within an inaccessible office, you stood by me through thick and thin, providing encouragement and understanding during every shift. Your compassion and inclusivity have made a lasting impact, and I am forever grateful for the memories we shared.

I want to say a very special thank you to Clare Thomas for believing in me as an author and a person. For taking a chance on me and giving me her unwavering and immeasurable support and guidance from the first day we met. I cannot thank you enough for helping me realise my dream of becoming an author. You have not only made me a better person, but with those countless hours of us talking about why I wrote Max and the Magic Wish, you helped and pushed me into thinking about why I wrote the story and made me realise that deep down, the story is a true one of self-acceptance and is one I need to continue to go on if I am to fully accept myself as a disabled person. Clare's talents are endless, especially when it comes to illustrating. The characters in our children's book are truly magical, and I thank you for your hard work creating them. Thank you for publishing these two amazing children's books, including Paddy the Polar Bear Teddy. I am so grateful to be able to call you a special friend, and I'm thankful the stars aligned and brought us together on a unique journey.

Lastly, I can't thank you all enough for embarking on this amazing adventure with me! To all the fantastic readers who have read my children's book and helped me make a difference by showing little ones that it's okay to be accepted and accepting of others, you've filled my heart with joy and laughter. Your support means the world to me, and I'm thrilled that my stories have found a special place in your little ones' imaginations.

To every one of you, thank you for being so awesome! Your kindness, enthusiasm, and open heart made this journey more joyful and meaningful than I ever imagined. So, let's continue this adventure together. I am eternally grateful for your love, laughter, and the unforgettable memories we've created.

Gavin

"The only disability in life is a bad attitude."
— *Scott Hamilton*

CONTENTS

INTRODUCTION	1
1. The Son	5
2. The Brother and Uncle	31
3. The Pupil	52
4. The Sportsman	87
5. The Workingman	114
6. The Songwriter	140
7. The Author	157
8. The Sceptic	181
9. The Misunderstood Man	201
10. The Joker	237
11. The Lover	250
12. The Friend	255
13. The Future	270
14. Hope	277
Also by Gavin Clifton	291

INTRODUCTION

The world is a unique and sometimes challenging place to live, explore, and navigate, and not everyone looks, behaves, or thinks the same at any given time or period. However, we can sometimes become influenced by certain factors like cultural norms, what we see in the media and on social media, generational expectations, and even celebrities or influential individuals.

You could say we are permitted to roam and live on this planet for our chosen time. Who decides this has been debated for centuries. Is there a God? Or is there some realm of superpower in a galaxy far away driving the Big Bang theory that decides the universe's and our fate? The truth is, nobody knows.

Still, I do know that whatever we all do in life's journey, the experiences we endure and the memories we make mean that whether we choose to tell them or not, we all have a personal story, and sometimes more than one.

Some of the topics I talk about in this book will take you on an arduous, emotional, funny, eye-opening, and sometimes what may be perceived by you as a reader as a subjective journey. We are all entitled to our opinions on how we want to live our lives. I get that. But we only learn and adjust our paths by making mistakes and judgements. We are all entitled to our own opinions and choices, and with every choice I have made thus far, whether bad or good, I have learned from whatever actions or consequences come from those actions and intentions and kept on navigating life's journey the best I can.

I can be impulsive, and you'll probably sense a little bit of that impulsiveness in this book because I do, in some parts, ramble on about various factors within a short space of time. Still, it's how I feel it's best to get my point across, and honestly, it's how I am in life in general, but having a speech impediment, this is how I've been able to express myself by sometimes being one hundred miles an hour and expressive.

I have also caused a few contentious situations on one or two occasions. I am very protective of myself and those who mean a lot to me. But still, I want to put on record from the beginning of this book that nothing I have written is directed at anybody in particular because, being different, the relationships you build with other people give you the strength to never give up and keep going. These differences, flaws, and mad and vulnerable moments are the times and things that make you realise and accept that it's best to make allies and not enemies, especially with the people who accept and love you the most. Life is too short to hold grudges.

My story about living with cerebral palsy is a unique one. Still, I want to use it as a catalyst to inform and educate everyone about as many aspects of my experiences as possible and show that despite having differences, you can follow your dreams, become competent, sometimes independent, and lead a successful life. I respect that my journey, experiences, and values may not agree with everyone. Still, if my story resonates with some, this journey is worth the miles, sweat, tears, anger, frustration, smiles, bad times, good times, and achievements.

Whatever you take from this book I hope you stay engrossed enough to read my story from cover to cover and not throw it on the log fire or use it to prop up your broken bedside table leg, which I'm sure you won't (fingers crossed).

I want to make a difference and give you a personal insight into my world of disability. Still, at the same time, I want to stress that I realise that while we advocate for a more inclusive and accessible world for everybody, we are making strides to make it a better place to live. Although the likelihood of society becoming fully inclusive and accessible in my lifetime and far beyond is a reality that is still a long way off, a lot more needs to be done before we can achieve this.

But what I can do in my lifetime is give hope to not only others with disabilities but also parents of children with disabilities and people in other areas of society that we can build a world that recognises the immense potential within every person, regardless of their abilities, and create a future where barriers get replaced by realistic possibilities within each person's capabilities. Hopefully, I can empower this realisation of a more outward-looking and thoughtful world throughout this book.

Thank you for picking my book up and reading it!
All my love,
Gavin

CHAPTER 1
THE SON

"My advice to other disabled people would be, concentrate on things your disability doesn't prevent you doing well, and don't regret the things it interferes with. Don't be disabled in spirit as well as physically." —**Stephen Hawking**

June 1982—a crucial time in my family's history I was born, among some other important events!

Ok, here goes. I need to start from the beginning and tell you about that significant time in history when the first child of the Prince, now King, and the then Princess of Wales was born. But that wasn't the only momentous moment that occurred that particular day—well, not at least for my parents anyway. It was the day I was born and the start of a journey of fight, survival, acceptance, and pain.

My mother gave birth to me at The Royal Gwent Hospital in Newport, South Wales, UK, just before Lady Diana gave birth to Prince William on Monday, June 21, 1982. Can you tell the uncanny resemblance between us? The big ears and receding hairline? To this day, I tease my mother and claim William and I were swapped at birth somehow, even though we were born miles apart, and that I'm the real Prince. I was the closest baby born to Prince William, and we received A Royal christening robe in the post, which I was later christened wearing.

On a hot and sweaty day in June 1982, my mother went into labour with her first child, but little did my parents know what lay ahead. Having your first child is life-changing for any parent, but being told that your child will likely not be average during its first agonising living hours is traumatising. While lying on the birthing table and enduring the excruciating experience of giving birth, it soon became apparent to the midwives, nurses, and doctors present that there were to be serious complications. Ok, you could argue that the stars were aligned, my fate was sealed, and I was to be a stubborn soul from the word go! It must have been warm and cosy growing in my mother's womb, so much so that I wanted to stay in there. Why dive-bomb into a parallel universe unknown to babies onto a cold and hard hospital bed when you can stay somewhere safe and get fed almost twenty-four-seven?

As my mother was in full flow, huffing, puffing, and pushing with her modesty, all gone southward, the medical team's expectant joy quickly turned to a high degree of concern. Instead of seeing my head there, ready in the birthing position, prepared to pop out and say hello, they saw a little red-rosy backside. Without any warning, I was born breech. As I often joke to everyone when explaining how and why I have cerebral palsy, 'I came out into the world arse-first or ass-backwards.' I bet you've already questioned my sense of humour during the short reading of this book. Oh, there's plenty more of that to come.

My entire birth was a long and natural one. Well, except for mooning the doctors and nurses with my rear end. The medical team chose not to perform a caesarean on my mother or use forceps. However, I wasn't breathing at birth and continued not breathing for some time afterwards.

Mum has in the past shown me photos from when I was in the incubator, and to now see how ill and close to death I was in the first seconds, minutes, and hours of my life puts how far I have come and what I have achieved so far into perspective. It could have been a completely different story. I could have died without the 'nurses and doctors' expertise, knowledge, and loving care. I wouldn't be sitting here now writing about how I have lived with and coped with cerebral palsy.

From the start, my mother experienced many difficulties when giving birth to me, meaning that the oxygen levels going to my brain dropped to almost nothing. It was touch-and-go. Going through the euphoria and excitement of having their first child should be a wonderful experience for parents. My father, unfortunately, witnessed his wife and child going through a lot of distress, which must have been terrifying. Not knowing if both mother and baby would survive through the first minutes and hours of your baby being born must have been mortifying for my dad.

Straight after my mother gave birth and received the aftercare she needed, doctors rushed me into intensive care for the first three weeks of my life, where I had around-the-clock attention. Even throughout these first risky weeks, it was still touch and go as to whether I would live. My oxygen levels weren't rising, and I was on oxygen support for a while. But, because of the brilliant care I received, I pulled through, and after around a month and a half, I was allowed home.

But this was just the start. Many doctor and hospital appointments were to follow for the foreseeable future. As you can imagine, there were many doctor visits, home visits, and hospital appointments I had to go through. Finally, after many tests and consultations, I was diagnosed with cerebral palsy eight or nine months into my life. This information was quite something that my parents had to take in and adjust to moving forward. I can only imagine the fear and mystery of the unknown and not knowing what lies ahead. When you think about it, this was forty years ago, and the medical knowledge and advancements weren't as clinically advanced as they are nowadays.

CEREBRAL PALSY STATISTICS

According to cerebralpalsy.org.uk, one in four hundred babies born in the UK has cerebral palsy. According to the most recent

Office for National Statistics in the UK, published in 2015, an average of 1,800 babies are born daily in England and Wales. In addition, about 1,800 of those children are diagnosed with cerebral palsy every year, equating to an incidence rate of around 1 in 400 births. According to cpsport.org, approximately 160,000 people have cerebral palsy in the UK, equating to 130,000 adults and 30,000 children.

WHAT IS CEREBRAL PALSY?

Cerebral palsy is a term used to cover several neurological conditions. These conditions are caused before, during, or shortly after birth as a result of injury to the brain due to any of the following reasons: limited or interrupted oxygen supply to the brain, a bleed within the baby's brain, a premature or complicated birth process, the mother catching an infection whilst pregnant, or changes in genes that affect the development of the brain. Sadly, in my case, there was limited oxygen to the brain during birth. Well, I did decide to come out 'arse-backwards' after all.

Cerebral palsy can affect muscle control, coordination, tone, reflexes, posture, and balance. Often, a person with cerebral palsy will display signs of the condition. Still, the effects can vary significantly from person to person. I experience all these, and yes, my balance gets greatly affected after a few pints of beer, along with some temporary memory loss (usually after around the fourth pint).

THERE ARE THREE DIFFERENT TYPES OF CEREBRAL PALSY.

• Spastic Cerebral Palsy (this affects muscle stiffness or weakness).
• Athetoid Cerebral Palsy (this affects muscle tone, causing involuntary spasms).
• Ataxic cerebral palsy (this affects balance and coordination).
I suffer from a mixture of spastic and ataxic cerebral palsy the most.

CEREBRAL PALSY AND A FEW 'ADD-ONS'

Along with being diagnosed with cerebral palsy, I also have a cleft lip and cleft palate that developed due to further complications while growing in my mother's womb. It was as if the hand of God, not Diego Maradona, but the one you see in the movies with a big hand coming down from the clouds, had decided my fate from when I was conceived: 'Yes, you're it. You are the chosen one. Cerebral Palsy, and a few 'add-ons, it is for you'; although, as far as I know, there is no direct correlation between cerebral palsy, cleft palates, and cleft lips, still, referring to the NHS.uk website, dental and speech problems are related to cleft and harelips, and I suffer from both.

    I later developed epilepsy, which meant I had quite a few seizures up until around four years old, which, as you can imagine, was a horrifying period for my parents. I honestly can't remember much from my personal account of having my seizures. I only vividly remember biting my tongue as I came out of my episodes and then having a numb sensation in my mouth and my tongue sore from where I had bit it. After that, I remember nothing else about my seizures.

Until I was ten years old, I was still under specialist care and had regular consultations. I was prescribed medication to control my seizures, and I had to take five pills daily. Two in the morning, one with my lunch, and two again before I went to bed. The lunchtime one proved quite tricky because, as I got older and started to go to my friends' houses and socialise, Mum often had to come and find me and make sure I took this pill to control my seizures. But thankfully, as I grew older, my seizures stopped, and the medication started controlling my epilepsy. A specialist, whose name was Dr. Ferguson, said,

"Gavin, you're doing so well controlling your epilepsy. I think it's about time we gradually wean you off your Tegretol medication to see if you can control it without medication". My doctor gradually reduced my pills until I wasn't taking any. After a few months of taking no drugs, Dr. Ferguson finally discharged me from his care, and, touch wood, I have been epilepsy-free ever since.

I was around a year old when the hospital consultations for my cleft palate intensified, and I eventually had my first operation to close the hole that had developed in the roof of my mouth. It is known as a cleft palate, a gap in the upper top of the mouth. This gap exists because parts of a baby's face didn't form together in the womb. My hole is still there, but it's tiny, and even to this day, when drinking hot liquids or even the odd smooth ale, I get remnants of that particular drink flowing up and out of my nose. It looks and feels like Mount Vesuvius suddenly decides to awaken from its sleep and wants to cause havoc with the hot or fizzy liquid I am drinking, finding its way up through the tiny hole in the roof of my mouth and exploding down through my nostrils just like lava spewing out of a volcano into the atmosphere.

If you see me on a night out, my eyes are watering, and I'm quickly wiping my nose or spitting beer over everyone. I've had a leakage, that's all.

MY FIRST CLEFT PALATE OPERATION

I went into the hospital and had the procedure on the day Star Wars: Return of the Jedi premiered. I remember nothing about this because it was so long ago and I was so young. Still, I now talk to my mother about that period and how she managed to feed me as a baby and toddler.

"I couldn't feed you a baby bottle with a normal teat. I had to use a special spoon and teat to ensure you were getting enough milk and feed it to you to enable you to develop sufficiently. I can only say that it did you well because nowadays you can't stop eating." Mum explained.

Not long after I had come out of the hospital after having my cleft palate operation, my consultants and surgeons turned their attention to repairing the gap that had developed in the centre of my upper lip. This gap is known as a cleft lip and is linked to the cleft palate, where a gap or split forms, in this case, in the upper lip. It's like a mini-earthquake has happened in the bridge region of your upper mouth, causing everything to collapse. This meant I was soon back in the theatre, having my first cleft repair procedure. Again, I have no memory of how this operation went because I was so young. Still, I will never forget the ugly, horrible scar it left me with for many years.

Admittedly, during my younger years, it didn't bother me that I had a visible scar on my top lip. Still, during the later years of secondary school and adulthood, the anxiety about having a visible scar in such a prominent position on my face started to affect me mentally. The pupils asked questions more frequently. Sometimes, I would ask my parents if I could skip school. I told them I wanted to see a doctor to explore the options of having this terrible-looking scar, or friend, as I called it, removed or repaired even further.

After an initial conversation with my doctor, he happily agreed to refer me to a face and scar consultant at Morriston Hospital in Swansea. After numerous consultations, the consultant surgeons mapped out the best way to get my upper lip looking near normal. I'm so happy that they did because I am much happier with my appearance now. Still, when I was twenty-one, this second cleft lip operation happened.

The only downfall was the aftermath because I had so many stitches around the lower part of my nose, nostrils, and mouth. It looked like my face had been through a sewing machine, and I was cross-stitched like an old antique teddy bear. If you had taken me on the Antiques Roadshow while my upper lip had stitches, I could have been sold for a fortune as a rare human novelty teddy. Every time I made a slight movement, my stitches would pull the skin in and around the area where the surgeons had stretched the cartilage and muscles on either side of my previous scar to make it smaller. The pain I experienced at this time was like no other pain I've experienced before. It was highly uncomfortable, but I could do nothing about the pain except take painkillers.

Furthermore, after this operation, I was taken to a room alone for a short while to receive the aftercare I needed before they put me straight into a ward where I wasn't comfortable. My anxiety started to creep in again as people looked at my upper lip. The swelling I experienced around where they had operated was unbelievable. It was like they had cut a tennis ball in half, suctioned it on my upper lip, and stretched my skin over it.

Being the crazy soul that I am, I phoned my dad to come and pick me up after having quite a, let's say, rather heated conversation with the consultants and nurses and then signing myself out of the hospital! Yes, you've read this correctly. The consultants eventually agreed to let me go home if I waited for them to assemble a medical package. I kept my stitches and wound area clean.

In all fairness, my wonderful mother cared for me twenty-four-seven until my upper lip had healed and it was time to return to Morrison Hospital and have my stitches out. I'm delighted that my last operation on my cleft lip all those years ago was a big success, and I wouldn't change a thing or go back. Still, my honest and heartfelt advice to anyone facing this type of surgery or parents with children with cleft lips is to have these correction procedures as early as possible. The older you get, the more risk you face and the more pain you experience. Let's face it: children are more forgiving and resilient to hurt and can move on and recover quickly. Plus, you can comfort them a lot more.

MY MUM

When I bring up the general conversation about having a disabled child from a parent's point of view and how they must feel about it, it's never easy. Looking at it from a disabled son's point of view, you get all kinds of unnecessary thoughts going through your mind, like, would they have loved me any more over the years if I wasn't disabled? Or I bet they wish I were normal. Look at all the pain and hardship I've caused them.

But, now speaking as a forty-year-old disabled man and still a bloody nuisance, I'm told by many that these thoughts are natural; I will never tell you any different. These thoughts were and still are sometimes caused by anxiety and over-thinking about the fact that I look different, when I now know that there's no need to think this way because it's ok to be different. Always be yourself, and if others can't accept you as you are, so what? The genuine friends and onlookers who do so are the ones who'll be there for you.

Mum tells me that as soon as she gave birth to me, all she could think about in her conscious mind was, why us? Even now, thinking about this personally, the sense of uncertainty she must have felt must have been mentally draining. Well, let's face it, it must have been a very frightening experience, seeing me rushed off due to complications and not knowing if I was ok.

Things would have been different if, in any way, they had known I was to be born breach. Nowadays, with ever-advancing technology, babies and their positioning are continually monitored. Of course, nothing is 100% unpreventable. Still, using these methods, early interventions could reduce the stress and suffering within the womb, perhaps in the long term. Still, what will be, will be. We are faced with the cards we are dealt, and let's face it, watching a baby develop in a womb would be ten times more watchable than watching Big Brother on TV.

Mum now also says that the best way for families going through the same experiences we did in my early years is to trust their intuition, and their maternal instincts will take over and lead the way.

"We just got on with life like any other average family. That's the only way. You learn on the job. It may be much more complex than most other families, but you'll get there. Just look at how you turned out. We did it!" Mum said.

After some initial post-natal depression, Mum says that a special bond began forming when she held me in her arms for the first time. My parents tell me the main challenges came from specific barriers we couldn't control. Like the authorities wanting to send me to a 'special school.' Mum could see I was starting to learn basic toileting proficiency. She claims she potty-trained me the same as any other toddler (that's not precisely true because she made me watch Top of the Pops and Sesame Street while I learned how to pee sitting on the potty). That's a strange mixture of daytime TV, I know, and I grew out of nappies quickly.

My basic academic skills were present. I was bright and could distinguish between the primary colours, count blocks, and tell you any animal you would show me. This is why my parents fought for me to attend mainstream school with the help of a nursery nurse. I'm so glad they did because I finished my schooling, passed a few exams, found a job early in my twenties, and have written two children's books. Mum has told me how proud she is of my achievements. Telling my story to help and advise parents and others with disabilities like cerebral palsy justifies my parents' desire for me to be mainstream educated all those years ago.

In addition, we were all invited by social services to go and visit other families who also had children with cerebral palsy, cleft palates, and cleft lips, and this was a great experience to see and learn how they coped. But we got on with it the best we could, keeping up with many appointments. As much as my mother experienced that initial post-natal depression, I can see now that it didn't take her too long to love me, just like any other firstborn baby, even though the scene was set. I've been a nuisance ever since.

Liz Davies, Gavin's Mother.

. . .

My advice for parents of children with disabilities is to go forward into parenthood with your eyes wide open. Where possible, do not always treat your child as "special." Do not give them too many special provisions. Admittedly, there will be times when you may have to stop them or hold them back from doing activities, but most of the time, treat them the same as any other child. Children only learn from making mistakes, which is no different for a disabled child. I was a little 'bugger' when I was younger but have done well with good parenting and the odd telling-off. So, 'learn on the job' and parent with confidence in everything that you and your child endure, and trust me, they will thank you later in life for making them the best person possible.

MY DAD

My dad often tells me he has only ever known me to be a fighter. From the day they were allowed to bring me home, my parents vowed to treat me as any other child, and with one or two exceptions, they have kept to their word and done just that.

"The early years were a roller coaster ride of emotions. We decided that Gavin would always be treated like any other child." Dad said.

Dad often reminds me that I thrived and excelled when participating in activities as part of a crowd, like being part of a football team. I still do now, especially when I go away with friends. You'll often find me joking around, and I'll discuss this later in this book. Ant and Dec have nothing on me when it comes to practical joking. This is the reason why I love to collaborate with others creatively, bouncing ideas off each other. It's one situation within a society where I feel included when working with other creatives.

Dad stands by his decision to have me attend a mainstream school because it made me the determined person I am today. Dad explains,

"If we had let you go to that special school the authorities wanted to send you to, your personality wouldn't be as strong as it is today. You wouldn't have had half the life experience you have had up until now. Your mother and I certainly made the right decision. Our trust in our parental instincts has been justified. I'm so proud of you."

From a personal perspective, despite being a lot older and having disabilities, I'm still my parents' son. Looking back on where we are today and knowing how much they had to fight for me to have the best chance in life is heartbreaking. It saddens me that, looking back in history, the medical and social models and representations of how they perceived and prejudged how a disabled child's whole life was to turn out are, in my mind, heartbreaking. I will discuss how I feel both models and the dialogue surrounding them affect the lives of disabled people later in this book. But essentially, as parents, they all want the best for their children, and always wanting the best for anything or anyone can lead us to make wrong or bad decisions.

Sometimes we learn by making mistakes, and sometimes our judgements can be wrong. Still, all disabilities are different. Some are physical, and some people have learning or hidden disabilities. Still, we all have the right to show our capabilities without judgement.

I want to thank my parents for quickly seeing how capable I was and still am. For believing in me and, most of all, for fighting for me to have a quality of life that medical professionals and authorities thought was out of my reach. As you read more of this book, you'll find out how wrong the authorities were, as I have defied most of these people from a social and academic perspective. As the Phil Collins song title goes, 'Against All Odds' (Take a Look at Me Now).

LEARNING TO WALK

Believe it or not, it took me seven years to learn to walk independently. Before this, I was energetic, loud, and into everything. I spent many years shuffling and crawling around our home, occasionally using our furniture as makeshift aids for support, a bit like Baby Sinclair out of Disney's television series Dinosaurs from the nineties. I loved it and used to watch it regularly with Baby Sinclair's signature saying, 'Not the Mama'. It was and is a classic.

I often got carpet burns on my knees, and in the summer, when I had shorts on, the burns only got worse. It looked like someone had taken bright red lipstick and coloured my knees for a cartoon sketch or an artistic project. This happened over thirty years ago now. However, during my neurophysical rehabilitation and physiotherapy sessions, I had access to professional disability aids and apparatus, such as parallel bars and walking aids. Unfortunately, my parents could not afford these professional disabled aids at home because they were expensive and still are today.

Undoubtedly, disability aids and apparatus were essential in getting me to walk. The support and sense of security you get when using this equipment are enormous. Training your brain to start working weak muscles is so complex and exhausting. Trust me. I know how hard it is. But sticking at it and not giving up on your body can be life-changing, so much so that I can get around unaided most of the time now. It has given me the joy of living a mostly independent life.

MY HOMEMADE WALKER

Disability aids and apparatus are expensive. They were all those years ago, so my father, a carpenter, bought me a wooden box with little wooden play building blocks inside. It was a toy for kids. He then fixed this box with four plastic wheels and an upright handle. He replaced the wooden play building blocks inside the box with a few house bricks to add weight to my newly adapted 'homemade walker.'

It took me some time to figure out that this walker was an aid to help me learn to walk. Still, eventually, I started to use it, first just standing on my two feet, holding the bar, and finding my balance. My mother would kneel behind me, now and again moving my feet forward, setting the rhythm and showing me what to do, one foot in front of the other, one step at a time.

As time went by, I learned how to walk. It took me a long time, but I did it, and as time went on, my dad would remove the house bricks one by one, decreasing the weight I was pushing against and lessening the weight as I got better at walking. As time went by, my confidence in my balance became more robust, and at the age of seven, I took my first steps unaided. And since then, I have never looked back.

"One day, we were at a car boot sale and came across an old-style walker for children. Only people of a certain age would remember these. I'll try to describe it. It was a wooden tray with four wheels and a metal handle that the child could hold onto. In the tray were coloured blocks of wood with numbers and letters. We had tried modern walkers, but all of them were too light and flimsy for Gavin, as he didn't feel safe with them and would cry and fall over. So, a purchase was made, and I took it home.

You're thinking, What's the difference? If you take the coloured wooden blocks out of the tray, the space is perfect for two concrete blocks. This made the walker very stable, and Gavin would hold onto it and stand. After a while, he grew more confident. Then came other challenges, such as taking off the braces so Gavin could bend his knees and feel safe without them. Gavin, the fighter he is, didn't give in and overcame any fears of falling. Then came stage two: I was to remove some weight from the walker. A concrete block was removed so the walker would move very slowly forward. The rest is history, as they say." Dad explained.

I DEFEATED THE ODDS. I WAS WALKING!

When I took my first steps, my parents were ecstatic, overwhelmed with joy and a sense of achievement. Still, this was so long ago now that I can't remember how I felt as I took my first steps. But it was a mixture of excitement and relief. Nowadays, I think back to before, after, and during my journey to walking. I always think of the running scene in the Tom Hanks film Forrest Gump and how he inspires others by overcoming limitations, and it's the story of how we all have something inside of us that gives us hope. Even if our triumphs and successes are small, they are the little wins. It's how we achieve them that makes us human and worthy.

Other people who were instrumental in helping me walk unaided were my grandmother, my dad's mother Maggie, who sadly died when I was a toddler, and Claire, my primary school nursery nurse. My parents worked then so we could have enough money for life's essentials and keep a roof over our heads.

Gran looked after me most days. Although I can't remember anything about her, people tell me she was a very determined and proud lady. She could sing beautifully, smoke like a train, and eat Fisherman's Friends as if they were Smarties. Maybe it's from her that I've inherited my stubbornness. She would take me for walks in my pram to the park, where I have also been told that she would take time out to hold me under her arms and try to get my legs moving. As you can imagine, they weren't all that strong. I was only young.

Mum tells me that when I was in primary school and in PE sessions during the early years, Claire, my nursery nurse, would work tirelessly with me doing simple physiotherapy exercises using the school's apparatus. As my legs got stronger, she would walk behind me and teach me how to step up and down the school stairs while I tightly held on to the handrail, pulling myself up and steadying myself back down them. Please remember that I am giving you an account of my journey here and how I eventually started walking. It was a long time ago, and times were slightly different than now. Paediatric and Neurophysical practices have advanced a lot since then. I know that everyone is different and that the complexity and severity of our disabilities vary, meaning some people cannot walk. I respect this fact. Still, I advise you to seek help and advice for your child as soon as possible.

Yes, how I learned to walk was slightly unconventional and crazy, but looking back, I wouldn't change a thing. I had and still have people around me who love me, believe in my abilities, and will always be there for me, no matter what. So, I'm curious if your children are going through the same things I did. All they need is love, encouragement, and a safe pair of hands to fall back on. Never give up on them.

MY ACHIEVEMENTS AND AWARDS

Because of my parents' decisions, I have won a few awards over the years. I won the most memorable award when I was around ten. In those days, these awards were called 'The Child of Achievement Awards', and they were being held at the Guildhall in London.

I was about to finish junior school and start comprehensive. If my calculations were correct, the year would have been roughly 1993. As far as I can remember, my headteacher, Mrs. Havard, a lovely lady, nominated me for this award. She was a petite lady and always full of life, and I remember her standing in as a teacher for my class for a few months of my last year of junior school. Unfortunately, I have yet to determine if The Child of Achievement Awards still exist or are called differently. All I know is that I won one.

They were prestigious events sponsored by some of the world's best-known companies or brands, and I still remember the year I won mine. A renowned fast-food company was supporting them. I'll let you guess which one. These award ceremonies are always star-studded events. The late Lady Diana presented me with the award, the then Princess of Wales, who unfortunately didn't remember or had no recollection of William and me being swapped at birth when I cheekily asked her who was her favourite Prince.

Still, as far as I remember, the after-party was fabulous, and I asked for many autographs. I was so star-struck. Some big names were in attendance. They were big celebrities back then. Cheryl Baker, Andy Peters, and Leslie Crowther were some of the people I met. Also this same year, I won a second Child of Achievement award locally within my County Council Borough, called Islwyn. The mayor at our local council office chambers awarded me this award.

RUBBING SHOULDERS WITH THE STARS

When I ask my parents about their memories of our trip to London and how the day went when I collected my award, Mum says that it was a surreal experience. It's not often you get to rub shoulders with celebrities and royalty. She tells me she's so happy and proud that I won a Child of Achievement Award, and every child at the event was there because of their achievements. We made the most of this special weekend. We travelled to London from Newport to Paddington by train, then were VIPs at a hotel she didn't know the name of. Still, it's opposite the Tower of London, where we spent some time on a tour.

The award ceremony at The Guildhall was grand, the room was big, and there were rows and rows of special and disabled children and families sitting at the front waiting to get on stage to collect their awards and certificates from Lady Diana, along with lots of celebrities and special guests. Mum particularly loved the after-party. I love being part of a crowd; I lapped up the attention, and my parents bought me a little red autograph book. I was tapping everyone, asking for autographs. I didn't care who they were. I just wanted to meet everyone. I'm still the same nowadays, weirdly and randomly saying hello to people at events.

Events like the Child of Achievements Awards still happen today, and rightly so. By receiving my award, I want to use this accolade as a token of hope, not pity, like some people see these events as portraying. They are entitled to their opinion, but I have never seen events like these as pitiful. Still, I see these events as hope not just for me but for the mums and dads of today who are doing an incredible job raising disabled children. It may feel like you could be doing a better job, but you are doing fantastic work, trust me.

I see these as opportunities to advocate for and educate the wider society about how we can accessibly and even socially change all walks of society to become more accessible, understanding, educated, and diverse. We can become much more inclusive. Even now, I'm forty years old. I'm still proving people wrong, like I did back then. It's why I received the award, after all. Remember, the unnecessary barriers around us make disabled people's lives much more complicated than they need to be.

SCHOOL ROLE MODEL

This may seem small to some people. Still, another of my accolades was being chosen to be a prefect in my final year of secondary school, for which only a few select pupils out of the year were chosen. A school prefect is an older student who becomes a role model for the younger students. Still, some of my crazy decisions may not fall into the 'role model' category, but don't tell my old teachers this.

There were a few other younger students at school with disabilities. I inspired them to enjoy school life responsibly despite facing barriers such as inaccessible classrooms and stairs within our school, which sometimes meant studying alone. But I didn't let this stop me from getting on with my everyday school life. For example, I can climb most stairs. Even nowadays, if there's no lift available, I try to use the stairs, even if it takes me longer than non-disabled people.

Back in my school days, if physical education lessons were too physical in the literal sense, a lesson subject consisted of playing full-contact rugby; I would play table tennis with someone else. I did feel left out because I couldn't play rugby with the non-disabled pupils due to my disabilities. I would have loved to go back-row forward or in the centre, but it wasn't to be.

Upon becoming prefect, I received enough nominations to stand for election to become the school's Deputy Head Boy, which was a massive surprise. Knowing that my teachers and peers respected me and saw me as worthy of being Deputy Head Boy has been something I haven't forgotten and never will. *But it was never to be, and I didn't get elected.*

THANK YOU, MUM AND DAD

I'm always curious to know how my parents feel about how far I have come and what they think about what I have achieved.

They don't say too many words, but that's ok because I know they are proud of me. Well, maybe not so much on some of the spontaneous and crazy decisions I've made throughout my life; for example, going to Benidorm for a few weeks for some 'resting time,' when they fully know I'll 'party until the cows come home' despite having disabilities.

They have and will continue to worry about me, and **NEVER** feel easy until I get home, and that's fine. Even though I'm now in my prime years, forty is the new twenty, or so I've been told. It's normal for every parent to worry about their children, even when they become adults. Whether they have disabilities or not.

Through love, dedication, and determination, I am so lucky to have parents in a position to fight for me to have the life I've had and the life I'm living now. Still, looking at the broader picture, we are fortunate to live in a wealthy country. It isn't easy because there are many other countries where children don't have access to the things we have in this country and are living with no food, in poverty, or even through war. Still, there's so much more this country needs to and can do to make the lives of disabled people easier, more accessible, and more inclusive. Because of all my parents' hard work, I have become the strong-willed person I am. They fought for what they believed was and has been the everyday life I needed to live. They've achieved it, and I love and thank them with every inch of my soul for doing so.

So, to set the scene for this book, the odds were stacked against me from day one. From being born 'arse-first' to needing help to take my first breath, I'm alive—still a nuisance that speaks his mind. Sometimes, I am a little stubborn and determined. Although it was unclear how disabled I would be for the first weeks and months until my diagnosis.

From day one, ableist barriers were built around me. Ableist obstacles in the form of the uneven landscape around us, stereotypical and outdated attitudes, fear, anxiety, lack of funding, inaccessible buildings, venues, and open spaces, a lack of disability awareness, and even arrogance, have been overcome through sheer willingness and determination throughout the last forty years. I am now living in the moment, achieving another dream, and owning my life by finally telling my story of how I have lived with cerebral palsy so I can show and educate a wide range of people out there that, with hope and with help, people with disabilities can independently, co-independently, and successfully live their lives if we can become more inclusive as a society. Still, many ableist barriers must be removed before we can move anywhere near becoming a disability-friendly society. It's time for a change.

CHAPTER 2
THE BROTHER AND UNCLE

"A hero is an ordinary individual who finds the strength to persevere and endure in spite of overwhelming obstacles."
–**Christopher Reeve**

My mother was born and bred in Newport, and my father is a 'Valley Boy'. That's how we are known around here. I am no different. I have lived in our little village of Pentwynmawr, a small, close-knit community in the heart of the South-East Wales valleys, all my life. I was raised in a typical coal-mining end-terraced house from a young age, then moved into a bigger home just over the other side of the village when my sister and brother came along. Our new house backed onto the football field, and this would be where I spent most of my playing days. Conveniently, it was somewhere my mother could keep a distant eye on me while I could spread my wings like any other child.

I bloody love my little village. It has been the only place where I have genuinely felt accepted and part of a community. It's like a family within a family. For example, you always call your mother's friend 'Aunty Diane'. I'm known and seen simply as Gavin. That's a lie because I'm sometimes called 'the nuisance of the village.' I can't think why. I'm only a little exuberant while under the influence of the enjoyment of life 'vibes' and a bit of alcohol occasionally.

I grew up from childhood into my teenage years in the late eighties and early nineties in a much different world than today before things started to change. Back then, life was much simpler, and children were much less exposed to what was happening outside their little circle. Life seemed to be a lot more innocent and straightforward back then, before the days of the smartphone and when mobile phones were only starting to impact how we communicated. The days of using the house phone or landline to call someone were still part of our lives.

Suppose you went on holiday with a friend's family without your parents or on a school excursion. You would have to use a pay phone, or telephone box, as they were known to ring home by putting ten or twenty pence in the slot before dialling your house telephone number. I remember the first mobile phone my parents bought me when I finished school as a present for managing to sit my exams. It was a Motorola MR30 on the Orange network. It was the size of a house brick, as nearly all the mobile phones were so bulky in those days that they wouldn't fit in your trouser pockets, and you had to keep them in either a coat pocket or your bag. Eventually, they became much smaller when I upgraded to a Nokia 5210. I thought I was the kid on the block playing the game 'Snake' on those phones.

There were no DVDs or streaming services, just the good old VHS, where you could tape over old programs. My mother would often tape over 'Match of the Day' or 'WWE' with the following Monday's episode of 'Neighbours' or Top of the Pops. It would annoy the hell out of me.

MY GAMING DAYS

My first gaming console was an Atari VCS 2600 with the good old Pac-Man game, and for those who have never played Pac-Man, it was a classic. With you, the player, controlling an eponymous character through an enclosed maze, you had to eat almost anything in your way while avoiding the coloured ghosts. So, when Pac-Man eats the dots without getting caught, you advance to the next level; if a ghost catches you, it is game over.

Then I had the Sega Mega Drive, where I would sit and play Sonic the Hedgehog for hours. Gaming and computer consoles have advanced so much since I was younger. But, from a disability perspective and having cerebral palsy with the right side of my body being affected the worst, it had a significant say in how I played, so much so that I have completely fallen out of love with gaming.

My brother and older nephew were completely gaming-mad. At the same time, my brother is still wholly gaming mad, and now my oldest nephew is too. I fell out of love with it because of frustration. Years ago, all you had were joystick controllers, which usually had one or two buttons to push on a stick, which you pushed in the direction you wanted something that you were controlling to move. As simple joysticks are used for some people's coordination and even pressure, they can become challenging for people with disabilities. Especially after using them for an extended period, you sometimes become tired quickly and lose concentration, putting you at a slight disadvantage when competing against non-disabled players.

I'd never make a good building site operator, and I'd be knocking structural objects and walls down, not assisting in building them. I'd be a health and safety hazard at the touch of a joystick.

Then came the PlayStation and Xbox. Gaming controllers completely changed with the emergence of the gamepad. I found these extremely difficult to use because you have to use two hands now, and using a controller with two hands is so tricky for me. It tires me out so quickly that my right side gets painful, so I haven't picked up a gaming controller for a long time. Still, these days, I know how people's gaming has changed dramatically, so much so that it has become more inclusive.

Gaming has advanced so much that you can now compete against and interact with other gamers worldwide, which is a fantastic outlet for disabled people who can't leave home. It now means they can interact with so many more people, meaning they become a vital and even educational part of a vast and ever-growing online community. Also, so many different gaming controllers have been developed. Undoubtedly, with more advancement and development stages to come, the fascinating thing is that some controllers are now adaptive, which are much larger and more touch-sensitive. The buttons are large and generally domed-shaped for accessibility.

You now have virtual games where you wear virtual goggles, even if you find using your hands or feet difficult. You can still feel a part of the game by wearing these goggles. I haven't gamed for a long time, but thinking back, even though gaming controllers weren't as advanced and accessible as they are now, Playing computer games, whether sport-themed ones, action games, or, most of the time, educational and problem-solving games. These all contributed to my upbringing, and I learned a lot of essential life skills by doing so.

Whether we have disabilities or not, we all have different interests and hobbies. However, our physical differences can sometimes limit our activities. Remember, it's about inspiring and showing the world that despite having disabilities, you have the desire and innovation to participate in hobbies you are passionate about, so if you have a child who takes a shine to a particular hobby, whether physical or not, I would explore all options and how they could participate. Having hobbies and participating in them is an excellent pathway for people with disabilities to become and feel a part of a community and make friends.

I wouldn't be where I am now if, over the years, my parents had been too overprotective, so my advice to parents is to be innovative and find a balance where you can allow your loved ones not only to find their way together with your help but more and more on their own too. You just need to trust them, and they'll soon find their limitations and independence by living life and sometimes making ill judgements, just like we all do, unless you're as crazy as I am.

As with toys, especially action toys, my favourites were He-Man and Masters of the Universe figures like Skeletor. Even now, at forty-one years of age, the big kid in me wishes I had kept my He-Man figures as collectibles. Yes, collectibles; that's all. Not to play with. I know what you are all thinking. I have grown up, honestly!

The yo-yo was another toy I loved. Despite having impaired coordination due to cerebral palsy, you'd often find me tangled up in the string. I would turn into a human version of Pinocchio for a while until someone came and untangled me. Still, the notion of a plastic wheel-type object spinning on a string fascinated me.

TV and film wise, and moving on from watching Wham whilst sitting on my potty as a toddler, my favourite children's programme was Rainbow with the characters Zippy, George, and Bungle. Fast forward to my teenage years, and I remember watching the film Robin Hood, the Prince of Thieves, starring Kevin Costner, Christian Slater, Morgan Freeman, Alan Rickman, and Mary Elizabeth Mastrantonio. With the famous soundtrack "Everything I Do: I Do It for You", sung by Bryan Adams, it had been in the music charts for a while. At every school or children's football disco at my local social club, it would get played for a long time after its release. I would stumble onto the dance floor, puff my chest out, and sing my heart out. Sorry, Bryan, for ruining the song as I screeched it out at the top of my voice while standing in some Welsh social club.

FAMILY LIFE FROM THE START

As I've mentioned previously, I was my parents' firstborn. Then, some four years later, my sister Hollie came along, and a few years later, my brother Louis unexpectedly joined us.

From my experience, it is a certainty that any parent bringing up and caring for a disabled child alongside their siblings who may be non-disabled is bound to give more of their time and energy to caring for the sibling with disabilities. Whether or not their disabilities are physical or hidden, as a caring adult, it is almost instinctive that you endeavour to give them the best chance.

My father worked a lot when my sister, brother, and I were little to keep a roof over our heads. Therefore, our mother was very hands-on and somehow cared for the three of us, but my sister and brother knew and came to learn that sometimes I needed extra care. They just went along with it and accepted that they would sometimes get less attention than I did.

As time passed, my mother perfected her routine when caring for all three of us and adapted it to devote more time to my sister and brother. She needed eyes in the back of her head when the three of us were around because one of us, little terrors, was often up to no good. She often tells me now that her best trick for safely occupying me was to put me in my cot or sit me on the living room floor with as many soft pillows around me as she could find, just in case I decided to fall from a sitting position. She'd then put a newspaper or children's picture book in front of me, and I would either sit and try to read them or rip the pages out of them. But this is the best part: she also says if a newspaper or the children's book failed to keep me occupied, her 'back-up' and the mother of all tricks to keep me entertained for hours on end was to sit me on my potty. Still, with soft pillows all around me in case I fell off in mid-pee and then put a VHS recording of 'WHAM LIVE IN CONCERT' on the television, I would sit and watch them repeatedly for hours.

Despite my mother caring for me most of the time, my father played a role in a typical father-son relationship. Most Saturday mornings, he would work overtime at the local caravan factory and take me to give my mother a rest from juggling caring for me and devoting more time to keeping my sister and brother occupied. He would sit me on the edge of his workbench and hand me one or two toys to keep me entertained while he did his work. In the early years of my life, both my parents worked full time, and we lived with my nana Maggie until my parents could afford a down payment on a mortgage for our first house. My Nana Maggie died when I was very young, so I have no memories of her, but I have been told that as my father cycled to and from work each day, she would often sit me in the front window. We'd wait for Dad to come home.

Days out as a family were always fun. We went on family holidays and outings like any other family. I remember that up until around the time I turned a teenager, whenever we went on day trips or holidays, we took my wheelchair, so if we knew we would have a long day of walking, I would sit in it while my mother or father pushed me everywhere. The wheelchair was to save my legs from aching and getting tired, as much as I hated being in it because of my stubborn streak. However, I had no other option because my hamstrings would tighten up quickly when walking, which they do nowadays. So, my parents made me use my wheelchair so we could get around more rapidly and stay out longer.

I often get asked why I am sitting in a wheelchair on the front cover illustration of my bestselling children's book Max and The Magic Wish, and I'm often not seen using one these days. It is because this children's book is a true story based on that part of my life, and I now exercise weekly and get physiotherapy when my hamstrings hurt the most.

MAX AND THE MAGIC WISH IS A TRUE STORY

Staying on the subject of my first children's book, Max and the Magic Wish, most people don't know it's a true story. Its storyline is based on a family holiday, and you will probably get the feeling that family holidays were a big part of our childhood. They were, and at one point, we had a touring caravan that, for a long time, we had permanently pitched at a camping and caravan site called Cofton Farm in South Devon. It was, and still is, a great family-friendly holiday park with a swimming pool and fishing lakes. Max and the Magic Wish's storyline centres around this area.

On a day out to Dawlish Warren, I met a fortune teller, and this is where and when the story unfolds in the book. I won't go into great detail about what happens in the book because I was hoping you could find out by reading it. Do you see what I'm doing here? I'm dangling a little hook, so you'll consider ordering a copy from Amazon. I never miss an opportunity to slip in a cheeky promotional plug for my children's books.

But then, I will tell you one little funny thing about that day. As we were about to set off on our way and continue our walk on the beachfront, the fortune teller, who is featured in the story, called me back and handed me a piece of paper with six lottery numbers written on it. My mother put them on the lottery every Saturday for a few years. But for one reason or another, the paper went missing or was thrown away, probably by mistake. There was no internet lottery in those days, so we threw the tickets away after each draw. Therefore, we stopped doing the lottery, or, more to the point, we stopped doing those numbers.

Thinking back, who knows if I would have continued doing those lottery numbers now? I could have been a millionaire, sailing the seven seas on my luxury yacht.

We always did fun activities as often as possible when my parents could afford them. Like going to the zoo, the funfair, or the odd activity centre like the ones with high and long slides leading down into deep ball pits. As children, we loved going down these slides, and I was no different. The only fun activity I couldn't participate in was swimming, and this is because I can't swim. Admittedly, my mother or father always needed to assist me, but they never stopped me from participating in these activities.

We did them as a family, and we had so much fun. Of course, we would get odd comments from other families for sometimes being slower than normal when doing activities such as climbing and going down slides. Still, we got on with it and made them wait. That was how we dealt with these situations. Every child has the right to be playful, and I was.

My advice to other families using any large-scale activities or even fairground rides is to, when there's a family with a disabled child taking a little longer to use them, be patient and wait your turn. Manners cost nothing.

GROWING UP WITH MY SIBLINGS

I ask my sister and brother what they remember and how they felt about the times we had growing up; my sister, Hollie, tells me that even though I have cerebral palsy and a speech impediment, I am still her big brother, an uncle to her two daughters, Isabella and Esmee, and a complete nuisance. My personality eventually always shines through, and my disabilities become secondary, she tells me. Being an uncle to my sister's and brother's children, where my brother has two boys called Jaxon and Deacon, is the best role in the world.

When I asked Hollie to give me some thoughts on how my nieces feel about having a disabled uncle, she said

"Whenever my husband and I are working and cannot pick the girls up from school, Gavin always steps up with my mother to pick them up and wait until their father or I get home from work. When Gavin isn't around, the girls are now at the age when they ask many questions about everyday things, including their uncle's differences and disabilities. So naturally, I answer these questions truthfully and honestly in an educational way, the best I can and to the best of my knowledge. This way, I know the girls are getting the best possible understanding I can give them about why and how Gavin has cerebral palsy, how it affects him, and how he copes with it, so when it comes to their friends at school asking the same curious questions that they've asked me, I know they have the knowledgeable answers to answer them accurately."

Knowing that my nieces see me just as their funny uncle is

heartwarming. As a disabled person, people will inevitably talk about my disabilities when I am not around them, and that's perfectly fine; I get it. However, if the dialogue they hear makes a difference and educates people, they can become more understanding about how disabled people live and work.

Hollie often reminds me that my disabilities when we were young were very much part of family life. We just got on with it. We naturally adapted to my needs, and we did cope. Admittedly, we needed to do certain things and activities differently, so I felt included, but so what? Life is a challenge for most of us.

We, as a family, just upped our game more and found intuitive ways to live life around my needs and aspirations, which are very high. She sometimes worries that I set my goals so high that sometimes I set myself up not to fail because 'failure' isn't a word in my vocabulary, but I set limits that even non-disabled people may not be able to reach or achieve. Hollie has often told me, 'As stubborn and crazy as you are, there's no holding you back. But unfortunately, I've failed to tame you over the years, and to this day, I still haven't convinced you it's time to slow down.'

I know deep down that my sister still worries about me, especially when 'I put on my crazy playboy act', as she puts it, and I know that she'd love to see me settle down with someone, eventually letting myself be loved by someone relationship-wise.

She says,

"I know Gavin has gotten used to being single or a bachelor. As siblings, we have spoken about how he finds it difficult to let his stubborn guard down when allowing himself to be loved. Still, I know that underneath his crazy playboy act, there's a loving soul inside him, and he can be in a relationship. He needs to look in the correct places to find a compatible companion, that's all. Still, I know that his nieces will always be on hand to help with anything he needs and even go on crazy nights out with him, if he's still as mad and capable when they both turn eighteen. He will always be loved, just the way he is."

Enough of that soppy talk; let's find out what my annoying little brother, Louis, thinks about having a disabled sibling. Being the family's baby, Louis got away with pretty much everything. But, like any other little brother, he'd torment my sister and me to our instinctive limits and beyond, and when Louis overstepped those limits, oh boy, he knew he was in trouble. He would push my buttons to the breaking point. We'd fight like cats and dogs.

Even though he knew I was different and had cerebral palsy. Louis would give everything, but in most instances, I would give as much as he gave me and sometimes even more. Hollie and Louis would lock themselves inside a cupboard or climb onto a wardrobe, so I couldn't get revenge.

Louis says,

"I once had a toy B.B. Gun. Not a real gun, honestly, but a plastic toy gun you loaded with plastic pellets. If you get shot with one of these pellets, they can hurt and even scar you. So, with me being the annoying little brother, I knew Gavin couldn't get away that fast or catch me most of the time. So, I would often aim at him, sometimes at point-blank range, and without care for which part of his body I would fire my pellets at, I would fire my pellets at him willingly, sometimes using the stair railing as cover. He would usually look like he had chicken pots afterwards. Then, after I had finished my full-throttle assault on him again, I would lock myself away for quite a while until he had calmed down and got over the fact that I had just gone all action man on him. These are childhood moments I'll never forget."

Those bloody plastic pellets did hurt. I was so frustrated; Louis knew I couldn't catch him. Good job. Revenge would have been sweet if I had Still, Louis is making the point here that, as brothers and sisters, we were no different from any other siblings in the sense of being playful and occasionally fighting like cats and dogs. We still sometimes argue as brothers and sisters, even though we are now adults.

Still, even though Hollie and Louis are now parents and have their own family lives, We do spend time together, and through living in a small village and having both been a part of the local football team, which I'll come onto later, Louis and I sometimes go on nights out together.

Louis says,

"Even nowadays, I only see Gavin as my big brother. Many of my friends and our intertwined social circle feel the same way. He always has and will continue to be 'one of the boys' and has always been included in most activities his disabilities allow him to, like nights out and football tours. From being with him in particular interaction situations over the years, for example, on nights out, looking from the outside in and from the point of view when people first meet Gavin, seeing his differences and trying to communicate with him can be daunting.

But what fascinates me is that with a little bit of help from the likes of myself or friends, Gavin can unknowingly make someone quickly forget that he's disabled, and I know that he believes that he's seen through a different lens by others. I've seen him go from a disabled person to a visible educator in society by being the focal point for sometimes intrusive questions in places that aren't meant for these situations. For example, he's naturally turned ignorance into normality on a club dance floor. Through the skill that only Gavin has, through simple words, answers to tricky questions, and elegant actions, he's turned a dance floor situation full of drunk people into a knowledgeable and fun party experience. Only Gavin is nuts enough to pull this off, and I admire how he does it.

Still, over the last few years, I have noticed that he is starting to feel more isolated because of friends moving on with their lives, settling down, and having their own families. But who knows what lies ahead? Gavin may still have a little family in the future because age is just a pointless number nowadays. But, for now, his drive and passion for writing and music and his desire to make a difference and advocate for a much more educated and inclusive society give him a massive purpose in life. Gavin always tells me he dreams of creating a sustainable pathway into the music industry for more disabled songwriters and showing how different technology can enable physically disabled writers to become known internationally and write hit songs. I can't wait to watch him grow as a writer."

CURIOUS CHILDREN

My sister has two girls, my nieces Isabella and Esmee, and my brother is a father to two boys, my nephews Jaxon and Deacon. I love them all to bits, and my relationship with my nieces and nephews is so joyous. From a very young age, they realised their uncle was a little different from other grownups, and they still ask questions about how and why I look and speak differently to others. I love that they, like all other children, ask many questions and are curious.

My sister and brother are so honest with them, which is fantastic because being honest with children early on is the best form of education. We always listen to and respect our parents and what they say. This is why every parent should discuss disabilities and diversity with their children as soon as possible. There is more and more information online nowadays, and even social media has its uses, with more disabled influencers creating content that advocates for and educates others on how to interact with and treat disabled people. These resources need to be utilised and watched in the home by families; incorporating this into a fun family get-together or activity is a great way to slowly start introducing young children to how, for example, our differences affect us. Two: how being hateful online can have lasting consequences for disabled people's confidence and mental health.

Seeing children innocently ask questions that adults shy away from asking makes me smile and sometimes laugh. I get so happy when our children ask those curious questions because this shows me that they aren't afraid of learning and spreading their wings. Disability awareness and education are vital to becoming more inclusive. Once we understand the essential medical, social, genetic, and health issues surrounding all kinds of disabilities, whether they are physical disabilities, hidden disabilities, learning disabilities, or even mental health issues, that's when we become more understanding of the different struggles disabled people face each day.

Still, I undoubtedly believe that moments of fear and not knowing how to embrace others are due to the lack of compulsory disability awareness training and education within the essential parts of society. These include social media, employment, retail, and the hospitality industries, which are at the forefront of our everyday lives. Could disability awareness become a core and compulsory subject of our curriculum where our children learn how and why we are disabled early on at school? Could disability awareness also become part of our hospitality and job inductions or training? Making people aware of the different types of disabilities and training them to interact with disabled people will make our retail and socialising spaces more accessible and make it compulsory for our retail and hospitality buildings and venues to make it easier to get around by installing ramps, lifts, handrails, and accessible toilets and changing rooms.

I LOVE MY ROOTS AND WHERE I'M FROM

All of the above is why I still live at home with my mother. Yes, that's right, I am yet to flee the nest. Let's be honest here. Having all your washing, ironing, and cooking done for you is a no-brainer when you are torn between staying with your parents or finding my place.

My mother and father separated years ago. I have always lived with my mother and her now-husband, Phil. I have forever had a close and co-independent relationship with my mother; she is just as barking mad as I am. This is the reason we get along so well. She often tells me to stay home with her for the rest of our days. I am happy to do so, but in the back of my mind, I know that one day, if I ever step out of my comfort zone and smash down the barriers and fears stopping me from being loved by somebody else, I would love to start my own family and have children.

Our roots, surroundings, upbringings, backgrounds, and family life all contribute to our lives and play many different and pivotal roles in shaping our journeys and moulding us into the people we eventually become. These help us lay the foundations and building blocks we cement in our designs over time. I swear by one rule and quote:' Our disabilities never define us. Although, for most disabled people, their disabilities stay with them forever. Society and how the world functions change constantly. In many ways, different ableist barriers are continuously placed in front of us because of the lack of thought, understanding, and educational disability awareness being put in place by the people and authorities that have a say on how we can accelerate our society into a more inclusive one. We have different, conflicting ideas from other people and organisations like the government, medical professionals, local authorities, teachers, friends, and families about how we live. We have a long way to go if we want to and can do so where disabled people rightly have more say in our lives, and we should be able to have much more say in what we want out of life without being questioned mentally or physically.

Despite all of this, I am my parents' son. I am still a brother and uncle who has built up a solid and unique family and social life and, with the support of my family and friends, has battled and still is battling through the many barriers that stop me from living the life I know I can. I have achieved so much, but with more disability awareness, education accessibility, and support from the government in areas such as communication and accessible spaces, who knows how much more I could have explored and done? Still, I am an example, living proof, and a beam of hope that with the love, support, and 'exibility' of having people around me who have supported me, even though there's so much more that needs to happen access- and awareness-wise, you can still find your way in life even with the limited tools and inaccessible areas that still exist for disabled people and prevent us from thriving and showing our worth. Still, moving forward and for future generations, I know there's enough intuition and hope for better things like inclusion, diversity, and a more accessible society for children and others like me with life goals waiting to be unlocked, unleashed, and put into practice. To reach those ambitions, we must put the past and our differences aside to achieve our potential.

CHAPTER 3
THE PUPIL

"Part of the problem is that we tend to think that equality is about treating everyone the same, when it's not. It's about fairness. It's about equity of access." —**Judith Heumann**

Let's talk education. I must have listened and learned something at some point, even though my attention span is sometimes less than a goldfish's. Still, I've done alright up until now.

I attended school a long time ago, and things have changed a lot within the educational system since then. The days of teachers retreating to the staff room for a quick 'calming cigarette' are long gone, where the aroma of nicotine would always linger whenever you walked past the staff room.

Throughout school, I could never get away with skipping

lessons and having a nursery nurse by my side. If I weren't in class for any reason, they'd soon enough send a search party out to look for me. In school time, more often than not, I'd play the 'I need to go to the toilet' card to get another few minutes' break from class. But, of course, you always get away with that one being disabled.

I often get asked if I went to school, and the simple answer is yes. My disabilities are physical and do not require learning, and I mean this in the nicest possible way. There are many types of disabilities, and each person with a disability has a unique personality. They also have flaws, just as I have my faults, but we all have strengths. It frustrates me when people make assumptions that I am not academically capable because I look different. It's a myth instilled into some but not all parts of society over many years through fear and a lack of knowledge and willingness to educate ourselves on how different types of disabilities can affect us. One of my favourite sayings is, 'Never judge a book by its cover.' Okay, you may have judged this book by its cover before picking it up, and in a good way, I hope.

Let's get back to talking about my education. I attended nursery, primary, junior, and secondary school like every other child. I believe every child deserves the right to an education, whether disabled or not. It doesn't matter how academically talented you are; access to an education is vital.

As a child, I had a lot of support. As a toddler and young child, learning support would come to our house and put me through my educational paces, making me do the essentials such as building blocks, identifying colours, and everything any child does in their early years. I picked up these essential skills quickly, and my parents could see that academically I was capable. Like any loving parent, my mother and father want the best for their children, and even now, it's no different.

From a physical perspective, it was clear that I needed a little assistance, which meant if I were going to attend school, I would need one-on-one support full-time. I was granted the funds for this. But, after many assessments and without consultation, the authorities decided that I was to attend a special needs school in Ebbw Vale, in South Wales, in the UK. Still, my parents could see and wholeheartedly felt that, developmentally and academically, a special needs school might not be where I could be challenged to my full potential. Hence, they decided to fight the decision made by the authorities with determination to the end.

THE FIGHT WAS ON, AND THE BATTLE HAD ONLY JUST BEGUN.

My father worked with someone who knew our local MP at the time. After telling this person about my situation, they told our MP all about it. They asked if they could help us fight the decision made without our consultation by the authorities. My father received a phone call a few days after this conversation with his work colleague. It was our local MP, and to my father's surprise, they asked if they could come to our house to meet my family and, more to the point, meet me personally.

A few days later, there was a knock on our door, and standing there was our MP and their assistant, so my father invited them in for tea, biscuits, and a chat, with myself being so young and none the wiser. I innocently played with my toys, building blocks, and colours. You could say I was ready for the fight and channelled my 'underdog Rocky Balboa' wise-guy New York-Italian talking character in my innocent way back then, even though I didn't realise what all the fuss was about.

Looking back, this was a blessing because our MP, without any doubt in their mind, decided to help my parents fight the decision made by the authorities to send me to a special needs school. Thus, we won the authorities over with persistence, and I was to have a mainstream education after all.

I look back now as a grown, academically capable disabled adult who has gone through full-time mainstream education. As someone who has previously held down a full-time job for over seventeen years and has successfully moved on to becoming a bestselling children's author, songwriter, and disability advocacy writer, I have mixed feelings towards the authorities. Part of me feels that I should throw a barrage of anger at them for initially wanting to send me to a special needs school. Still, when I really sit down and think back to the days when I was young, my parents' decisions were most probably made on the basis that they had less educational material and resources than there are nowadays to help them understand the severity of my disabilities and how they would shape my academic journey in both problematic and positive ways, like they eventually have done when you see how my life has been and is turning out to be. The people acting on behalf of the authorities only knew back then what they had learned and maybe didn't understand how to establish and see that I was academically and mentally able, and the complexity of the methods by which they determined this may not have been as researched, studied, and advanced as they are now. I am not your average person with cerebral palsy and have lived a co-independent life. I have been able to do more things than other people with different disabilities.

Even though this book's theme is education, raising awareness, and hope, I am always mindful that the spectrum of learning and physical disabilities and how they affect different people vary considerably. For example, someone may need to attend a special needs school based on their needs and safety. On the other hand, having a regular mainstream education was life-changing and vital to making me who I am now. Still, due to my physical limitations, I couldn't have gone through school without the one-on-one assistance I had in the form of a nursery nurse.

My one-on-one assistance began when I started nursery school. I had a nursery nurse by my side throughout my academic years. This kind of help and security were so helpful and played a vital role in my journey and in getting me to this stage in my life. In addition, having the proper care and support while I was in class took a lot of the worry out of getting around on my own. It allowed me to concentrate on my classwork one hundred percent of the time.

But there was a unique period during my school years when I struck a special bond with one particular nursery nurse, Claire. We clicked immediately and were inseparable and united, just like the A-Team was until my last day of primary school. I was even Claire's page boy at her wedding. We did everything and went everywhere together. Claire would be right by my side if I had any medical or paediatric appointments or swimming hydrotherapy sessions during school.

Claire attended my neurophysical rehabilitation appointments at Priory Mount Eveswell Clinic, Newport, in South Wales, UK, where I underwent physiotherapy and hydrotherapy sessions like swimming and motion and balance exercises. I even went there to get my plaster casts put on my feet and legs in preparation for splints, which doctors fitted onto my feet, ankles, and legs to help stretch out my lower leg muscles. I had many of these sessions throughout my primary school years, which helped my physical and mental development.

These days, these types of centres of excellence are predominately run and funded by charities. The children can now be referred to them by medical professionals, or parents can self-refer their children if they wish. Access for children with cerebral palsy must continue. Without this access, my development would have been left to my parents to source this vital rehabilitation, adding another challenging financial burden to our family lives. I wouldn't have been as capable and independent as I am today if I had been deprived of neurophysical rehabilitation back then, that's for sure.

I want to dedicate this part of my book to someone special who played a vital role in supporting me through primary school. My nursery nurse and sidekick, Claire I knew I needed to ask her to share her experiences and memories as a professional nursery nurse and now as a dear friend. Here is what Claire said:

MY NURSERY NURSE — CLAIRE TIPPINGS

"In 1987, I was invited to Pentwynmawr Primary School, where there was a possibility of a full-time post working with a young boy with cerebral palsy. It was my second post, and on our very first meeting, a special bond formed as we studiously worked through a math challenge looking at fractions. In those days, teaching assistants were called nursery nurses and worked one-on-one, unlike today in mainstream schooling. From that moment on, we were 'partners in crime' as we embraced life's challenges in our quest for acceptance in a challenging and ever-changing educational environment.

Gavin's characteristics were positivity, optimism, enthusiasm for life, sheer determination to be the best he could be, and the mindset to drive his ambitions. He was very much a teacher and taught me a lot, too. My ambition was always to use a positive attitude that made him believe he could be as successful as he wanted. Gavin's ambitious mindset gave him the positivity to push beyond expectations. He had a purpose and a goal to achieve in all areas. This commitment to his resilience inspired and helped his ability to adapt to situations, never giving up on his dreams.

Although we wear many different hats that allow us to be who we want to be, perseverance and commitment will enable us to control our destiny. We worked as a team. Hence, I am incredibly proud to have contributed to Gavin's life, enhancing and enriching the visible and tangible things. I also aimed to make Gavin's life rich in hope and determination to go forward with resilience and belief in his goals to be the best he could be in all walks of life. We did this through sheer hard work, using the processes of physiotherapy, hydrotherapy, occupational therapy, and speech therapy.

Ultimately, Gavin wanted to be the same as the other children. Essentially, by keeping extremely focused, the 'process' allowed Gavin to progress from doing 'bunny shuffles' (moving along on his knees with a shuffle, which caused many uncomfortable sores). Walking the flights of stairs from the infants to junior departments (which must have felt like climbing Everest) with sheer grit and determination. On many of these expeditions, Gavin would question why his legs didn't work correctly, to which I'd answer the truth (always the truth; honesty and respect played a considerable role in our relationship) that his brain wasn't sending messages to his legs. His desire to be mobile, be seen as the same as his peers, and fulfil his dreams was a testament to his courage and determination.

I loved being around this little boy who, for all the odds stacked against him, persevered with his physio activities on his Pedro ladder-back chair, wearing the boots that supported his ankles (but weren't cool in Gavin's eyes). We religiously worked on ongoing speech therapy programmes to aid others' understanding of how you expressed yourself—using the gadgets to overlay on the QWERTY keyboard. We became very good at using this tool as a way of 'bagging ourselves more time' on the only computer in the classroom, much to the annoyance of others. However, this tool proved to be invaluable to Gavin's future.

He set goals that scared him, but they pushed him forward. Setting goals was a positive way to take control of the direction we were heading. It was liberating when those moments were realised, like when Gavin was selected for the football team. He played the last 10 minutes of each match, with his classmates cheering with pride. Undoubtedly, Gavin wouldn't be accepted as part of the team, and his peers would be wealthier for the experience. We also went away for outdoor pursuits. Gavin stayed the night, something he'd never experienced without his parents. Like the other boys in the dormitory, he bounced on beds and ate midnight snacks. I kept a mindful distance, not to encroach on his space but to be there if needed (rather than wanted!).

I will hold dear to my heart the day my page boy stood through a very long wedding service, refusing any support—another testament to his courage and sheer determination. Gavin thrived on all these opportunities, always giving 110%, wanting to be better, and making me want to do my best. On reflection, I can say to be genuine, honest, and truthful when a child with a disability confronts you with a million and one different questions. We worked on what we needed but always found time to be consistent—no regrets; we embraced whatever negativity and failures came our way.

We actively used changes in behaviour and the educational environment to have a better perspective on respect, trust, and loyalty to keep moving forward, celebrating each success (and there were many) as we achieved it. Each path opened up the future. Life gets in the way sometimes—too busy and prescriptive—but we always found time to have fun and be happy, and this led to the drive and passion we both held to succeed.

I wouldn't be who I am today if Gavin hadn't enriched my life. From that first day on, we met the wonderful young man you have become. Thank you from the bottom of my heart."

Claire Tippings, Nursery Nurse, Gavin's Pentwynmawr Primary School.

I will allow my stubborn, tough-guy persona to be broken down (only for a little while, though, I promise). When I received Claire's testimonial, I broke down in tears, and memories of our journey within that particular part of my life came flooding back. It was like going back in time. Lots of people have played essential roles in my life. Still, that special bond I formed with Claire played a massive part in making me who I am today. Our time together throughout primary and junior school was fated and meant to be, and the universe's way of shaping my journey and will continue to do so.

MY NURSERY SCHOOL YEARS

My mother didn't decide to take me to play school, so my early learning years and education started in earnest in a nursery. My mother tells me I enjoyed my nursery years and loved playing with other children. From then on, I was a very determined little boy. To this day, I am still competitive, stubborn, and determined-minded, just not so cute and little anymore and bald. I have now lost most of my hair, which I inherited from my father. I often remind him of this in a good way.

My mother would drop me off at Crumlin Nursery whenever I was scheduled to attend, whether in the morning or afternoon sessions. The nursery was only a ten-minute drive from our home. Since I left the nursery many moons ago, my sister, brother, and, most recently, my two nieces have all attended the same nursery in the same building. It's lovely that we have all experienced the same early start in life.

My one-to-one assistance was granted to me when I started nursery, so I had the security of knowing I had support right from the start. My nursery days were long ago, although I remember certain things, like the little tricycles and the sandpit in the playground.

I remember these tricycles being yellow, and once my

nursery nurse had helped me sit on one of them, there was no stopping me. It was like competing in my own Tour de France, trying to push myself around the nursery playground.

Although my legs weren't all that strong at this stage, my nursery nurse would help me get onto one of these tricycles at the top of an inclined pathway with other outside play stuff splattered around like my favourite sandpit, rocking horses, and footballs. I would lift my legs until I rolled down to the bottom of the path, falling off occasionally. Still, with each fall, it prepares you for what lies ahead. Because you grow up with cerebral palsy, you fall over quite often. You can do nothing about this because poor balance and coordination are part of the condition. However little or big the reaction is, on occasion you'll fall; there's no stopping. One minute, you are in full walking mode, and then, within a split second, you are making the overturned woodlouse impression.

CEREBRAL PALSY INJURIES AND ANXIETY

There have been two occasions in the past. Until now, I have had only two significant falls. On other occasions, I've had a few cuts and bruises, but I'm used to having cuts and bruises on me.

The first fall was when I fell backwards down a short bank of rocks and grass, landed square on a sharp-edged rock on my coccyx and lower back, and severely bruised these areas. The other time, I tripped over a table, put my weaker right arm out to save myself, and broke my wrist. I ended up in plaster for quite some time. Cerebral palsy is part of who you are and your only choice. You can come to terms with the fact that this condition is a part of who you are, or you can go down the road of self-denial, continuous anxiety, depression, and loneliness.

I admit that there have been times when I could have given in and fallen into this trap. There are other aspects of my disability where my anxiety could have taken me down. I talk about this later in the book. When you look and speak differently, you sometimes overthink many things and make wrong assumptions. You see, hear, and look for situations that aren't even occurring and even think the worst, which is the opposite.

For example, I've been sitting in a café where someone has been pointing and looking at me. Immediately, my body goes into protective and anxious mode, overthinking the situation, wondering what kind of ableist comments or remarks they make, and having the last laugh. Therefore, I confront them to let them know how I feel and how hurtful and selfish their actions are. But they were discussing how inspired they were by seeing me get on in life and how they wanted to see more people like me in the community.

Then, these are the embarrassing moments you wish would disappear out of guilt. Still, they are moments you need to endure and experience because they remind you. Yes, ok, you have disabilities that, somewhere in your conscience, you want to tell yourself are because of maybe some punishment for an awful crime-filled past life. However, there is also no escaping the fact that people will talk about you or endeavour to put you down in every walk of life. There's no getting away from those Chinese whisperers.

Still, I now know that the number of good people in the world who want to support you despite being different far outweighs those who always try to take you down. Remember, we have as much of a right to live the life we want and to follow our aspirations despite having disabilities as everyone else. Our disabilities are only a tiny part of who we are, but they never define us or make us less worthy. Never struggle alone. There's always someone to talk to, whether it's your family, a doctor, or even a stranger. It's good to talk.

PRIMARY AND JUNIOR SCHOOL

So, moving on to primary and junior school, again, this was a long time ago, and it's difficult to remember every detail. However, I attended my local primary school in my home village of Pentwynmawr. Our village school sits in the heart of the village. It always amazes me how striking this building is, how its history has evolved over the years, and how it's become a part of my journey and played an essential role in getting me to where I am today.

The school building itself is imposing; it seemed enormous to me as a child. The school playgrounds, or yards, are vast, with high stone walls surrounding them. There are two yards, an upper and a lower level, and I am trying to remember my year group playing in the upper yard all that often. Instead, we'd hurry out every playtime and make our way to the far end of the lower play yard.

In my last two years of junior school, I could walk alone. Before this, I would either stay in class during playtime, or my nursery nurse or one of the other teachers would take me out to play in a pushchair. Along with different situations and interactions, this period in my life, especially spending hours in this play yard, paved the way to becoming socially active and put me in good stead for when I eventually moved to a 'big school' or comprehensive school.

THOSE MOMENTS OF 'WHY ME?' MADE ME DETERMINED TO WALK.

So, back to when I had to sit in a pushchair in the school play yard. It was so frustrating, and sometimes it got very lonely. As you can imagine, children love to play, run about, play tag, play football, hopscotch, and other lively activities, and at this stage in my life, all of this was just out of my reach because I was not able to walk. I was only young; there were tantrums, anger, tears, and confusion. I often thought to myself, and still do now, when I'm having a bad day, "why me?"

I watched all the other children innocently having fun, playing tag and football; all I could do was watch them. Experiencing times like these—times of wanting, jealousy, and wanting something so bad—can either make you doubt everything you are. Or they can somewhat strengthen you, push you on, and encourage you to improve. They can become springboards for pushing your limits. Watching these children play and run about made me more determined to try and become like them and walk. It was a trigger moment and a vital part of making me even more set on walking.

So, every day after school, I would go home and use the furniture and the walking aid my father gave me to push myself to unknown limits. They were unknown limits because nothing in life was guaranteed, and at this point in my life, being able to walk was not guaranteed. Still, my life changed forever on a momentous day when I was around nine.

In a spur-of-the-moment leap of faith, I decided to stop using our furniture as a safety aid and finally take my very first steps. Emotionally, I can't remember how I felt at that moment. It was all a blur. My mother was in floods of tears; witnessing me achieve something was to change my life, but looking back now, this was the best day of my life.

So, being able to walk has changed my life completely. It was slow progress with each new step I took. I remember that perfecting my balance was tricky. It was like being aboard a boat on a rough sea twenty-four hours a day until I found my core balance. I had to do something in junior school most toddlers learn to do before nursery. Still, I was doing it, and training your brain and body to do new movements at nine years old takes a lot of energy.

However, my new sense of freedom was life-changing, even though it had been an ongoing learning process for a long time. Going from people continuously looking down to interacting with you at eye contact level makes you feel even more part of what's happening around you. You feel more included and equal. Being able to walk opened a whole new world for me. I could play in the park with all the other children and even get around the play yard, even though my nursery nurse would watch me from a distance for a few months until my balance improved.

I STARTED TO FIND MY WAY

Now, I am able to walk. My circle of friends started to grow, and my hobbies began to become realities. Days in the school play yard now turned into participating in football games with the others, and we played football every playtime. From this point onwards, I slowly started to find my way, joining in with the other children, and this then meant not just having one friend whom I met in the same play yard every day as I included in the story of my first children's book, 'Max and the Magic Wish.' But it meant I started to make more friends inside and outside of school. I was becoming accepted for just being myself.

As I hadn't been walking all that long, let's face it, being able to walk after nine long years of shuffling along on my knees was a huge adjustment. Navigating my way around the school play yard was a little unsafe. Remember, at this point, I was still trying to master the art of balance. In addition, there are many hard surfaces in a vast play yard, and I could accidentally fall at any time.

Therefore, each time I played, I wore a safety helmet. I

looked like I was about to do twelve rounds with Mike Tyson, and heading a football was a doddle. But, looking back, wearing a helmet and looking even more different and feeling a little anxious about wearing this safety helmet was a small price to pay if it meant I had no head injuries if I lost my balance. I would have given Tyson a run for his money in any boxing ring.

So, my time at primary and junior school came around quickly, flew by, and is enriched by my past. They were fond years that I will never forget. This particular period in my life was strange; it was tough. When you look differently than what societal norms expect, your anxiety levels seem to go up and down; you worry about how you'll fit in, and you tend to overthink a lot. I talk about overthinking a lot in this book.

At the time, my parents wanted Claire, my nursery nurse, and my sidekick, all away through primary and junior school, to continue with me on my school journey and assist me at secondary school. But it wasn't to be. Newbridge Comprehensive School already had a nursery nurse employed and waiting to help me when I arrived. Her name was Mrs. Matthews. At the time, I was distraught by the fact that Claire wasn't coming to secondary school with me, and to tell the truth, I was so unhappy that she wasn't allowed; I tried everything within my power, not even going to secondary school first. My anxiety levels were through the roof.

NEWBRIDGE COMPREHENSIVE SECONDARY SCHOOL

Secondary school brought about a whole new set of challenges and a new way of life, and it was a big adjustment that took time and a lot of energy out of me. I had to get to know Mrs. Matthews and adjust to a new working method. With Claire, we had our routines. We had a special bond, and our trust was set in stone. So, on top of the euphoria of the unknown insecurities of starting a new school, I had to form a new working relationship with someone I had only previously met once before.

Until then, I thought Pentwynmawr Primary and Junior School was big, but moving to Newbridge Comprehensive dwarfed my previous school. It was at least five times bigger, with lots more classrooms, more teachers, and a hell of a lot more pupils from all over the local area. There were significant changes in the way I did things. Previously, I only had to navigate to one classroom and one play yard. Now, many more classrooms within other building blocks spread over a much larger area, which meant more walking. This environment was testing alone, even before I dealt with the sheer number of more inquisitive children staring at me.

At Pentwynmawr Primary, the classes were tiny, and everybody knew me and accepted my disabilities. Moving schools, I was starting to have children I hadn't met before being around someone who looked different.

There were few social media platforms, let alone mobile

phones, back then, so the educational content we have now never existed. I was the educator, disability-wise, and I could sense it again. All eyes were on me as every pupil in my year group assembled in the school's main hall, where we were placed into separate form groups to report every morning for registration.

Previously, my year group at Pentwynmawr School consisted of just six boys. It now had over one hundred pupils, a mixture of boys and girls. Unfortunately, the six of us attending primary school were split across two form classes. So there were me, Wesley Colyer, and Mark Davies in one, and Dean Phillips, Damian Matthews, and Justin Evans in the other. I remember our first few days, where we mostly stayed within our form class until we settled in.

My new nursery nurse, Mrs. Matthews, and I mainly sat at the front of the class, where we worked together in the first few weeks to find a workable routine that suited us both, from the simple things like where I'd like my pencil case and ruler placed on my desk to helping me underline words and even carrying my bag between lessons. All these were simple adjustments—still essential little things—that allowed me to concentrate on my GCSEs over the next five years. Mrs. Matthews carried my bag for me every day. It was heavy because I used a laptop in some classes. If I had to carry my bag, it would have been an extra exhausting burden and affected my ability to learn.

FINDING MY INDEPENDENCE

At break and lunch times, Mrs. Matthews left me to my own devices, and to be honest, on her part, it was the right decision. It allowed me to start finding my independence as a teenager. Even though disabled people need support daily, they must get the chance to do things independently if they can. At this stage in my life, I started to nurture the balance of living co-independently at school and home, with my parents also giving me the space to explore my emotional and physical limits.

At lunchtime in school, Mrs. Matthews would first take me to the canteen to get my lunch, and of course, my favourite was pizza and chips. Wesley Colyer, whom I have known since primary school, and a few others who I had then, during the first weeks of starting comprehensive school, began to become good friends and would then eat our lunches. Then, we would all go to the school library, where we would hang out and chat until lunchtime ended, leaving Mrs. Matthews to enjoy her lunch break with the other teachers.

So, during this period of my life, when I was starting to become more co-dependent and growing up, they were some of the best times of my life and played an essential role in who I am now. However, attending a mainstream comprehensive school had some barriers and challenges I had to deal with, and these challenges were a whole new world away from my primary school years. I have already talked about how much bigger my new comprehensive school was than my primary school. There was a lot more walking, more pupils, and in between classes, I sometimes had to leave my lesson early to get to the next one on time and avoid the hustle and bustle of the school corridors being rammed with people and navigating the crowds without getting shoved. Most people were courteous, but you get the odd thoughtless person trying to push past, quickly knocking you off balance.

Pushing happens in all walks of society and occasionally happens today. As I have already explained, having cerebral palsy affects your balance. So please be mindful that if you see someone with cerebral palsy trying to get through a crowd of people, give them a little extra space around them and a little extra time to get to their intended destination. I'm at the age now where I can feel my body starting to slow down, and in fact, I'm embracing the fact that I have to adapt and do things like walk from A to B at my own pace, especially somewhere on a trip away with my friends. I'm more interested in taking in the beautiful landscape around me these days or an interesting piece of culture in that particular place. I'll eventually find the people I'm with on the trip, even if they won't wait.

POOR ACCESS AND GETTING AROUND WAS HARD

In terms of getting around at secondary school, I just about coped, with help from Mrs. Matthews and my growing circle of friends, coupled with my stubbornness and desire never to give in. However, access at both of my schools could have been better. There were many stairs to walk up and down. There are few disability aids like ramps and handrails, no accessible toilets, and no lifts to the upper floors. Although things may have improved now, it was a long time ago when I attended school.

But I often think back, and poor access hindered my educational journey, which I could have done without. For example, could a lift have been the difference between me being on time or late to class? I could have had more ramps to make getting into certain school buildings easier. These are all significant and, yes, costly adjustments that need to be put in place, but from a disability perspective, they all help on a physical and mental level.

For example, getting to a class on time and simultaneously with the other children put me in a reasonable frame of mind. I felt ready and included, and it meant not missing the start of a lesson, a subject, or a vital piece of information you learn better by hearing it directly from a teacher. These are all adjustments that inevitably could be the difference between you getting lower or higher grades in whatever subject you are studying and impacting your further education, professional career, and even the rest of your life. Our learning and educational spaces must be fully accessible to give all disabled people the best chance of having the education they desire and are capable of achieving.

I couldn't have gotten through my academic years without a lot of support, and through school, I had a few different people supporting me one-on-one over the years, and I genuinely thank them all for being there every step up to the point where I finished my education.

MY GCSES AND LAST YEAR OF SCHOOL

I sat for my GCSE in 1998. I only passed some of them, but I am proud that I always tried my best throughout my school years and gave it my all. I am the type of person who excels when I'm physically doing something and learning on the job. I despise long periods of revising or studying. My attention span is concise. Could this be because I have suffered a brain injury, and it's something that comes with having cerebral palsy? Possibly?

I still need to highlight the importance of supporting people like me through their school years. It is vital and helps those individuals excel to the best of their abilities at school. Still, I hear stories of children needing more funding for help. It is heartbreaking and needs to change with additional funding.

Secondary school was the furthest I went in my education. Well, I did attend college for a little while. It was a few hours, and I was like a lost soul in the dark. I wouldn't say I liked every minute I was there. But, from this point on, I had no one-on-one support, and I would have found it very difficult to settle into further education without the support I had been used to for so many years beforehand.

Going from having help on hand every day at school to being on my own at college was like losing a big piece of my heart. This loss would significantly affect my ability to learn and work to the standards I was used to. My future would have been compromised, so I decided to drop out of college and take another path.

Studying at a mainstream school shaped my life massively. I learned a whole lot of life skills. For example, I learned to respect others. I learned how to structure my days. Being a disabled teenager around lots of other non-disabled children, I could educate other children that not only being accepted for who you are but also accepting others who are different is vital. I did this by answering many curious questions from other children every day throughout my school years.

Most importantly, during my school years, I made many friends with whom I still have I'll be forever grateful to everybody who stuck by me through the best years of my life—my school years.

Not only this, but I was also the educator just by being visible. Looking back, if I had gone to a special needs school, I would have unlikely reached the academic potential my close family and friends knew I had, I wouldn't have been as visible within society as I am, even now. From an education perspective, there needs to be more compassion and understanding that we may be physically different or limited, but with the right amount of support and knowledge of how and where the support is needed, we can help disabled people in their education.

I realise that some of our school, college, and university buildings are centuries old, and more modern buildings have been built since I left school. Still, accessible facilities must be put at the centre of a disabled person's needs. You'll notice that one of my key themes throughout this book is education, whether it's educational in the way of academic learning, how we make access to all walks of society better, getting more disability awareness into the areas where it's needed, or educating morally on how to treat disabled people within the everyday community. We are all entitled to an accessible education and life. You may not be the most academically gifted person in the world, but access to an education is vital.

I didn't pass all my exams, but I tried my hardest. I gave everything, which is most important. I am now living my dream of becoming an author and songwriter. I am taking life by the horns, and I am loving life. Remember this, everyone: always be yourself, never give up, and do what makes you happy. Follow your heart.

EVERYONE DESERVES THE CHANCE TO HAVE THIS OPPORTUNITY.

From a personal perspective, I now want to thank my parents, my family and friends, and our local MP for believing in me. Without their determination and fight, what would have been wrong decisions regarding my education could have changed my life completely. I want to highlight that I understand that everyone with a disability is different. Every disability is different, may it be a physical disability, a learning disability, or a hidden disability, and their educational journey may be a whole lot different from what mine has been. To have the opportunity to get out there and get the chance to be the best person you can be is everything.

Being disabled doesn't mean we can't follow our dreams. But I am a great believer that having an education plays a significant role in shaping our futures. Our aspirations become enriched by our destinies, and only sometimes by how well we learn from studying. Still, it helps, and having a solid education and the support I needed has guided me to where I am now, finally chasing my dreams of being a writer and author.

Of course, not every disabled child's educational journey will have the same outcome. Still, the right to have an education remains. If you are a parent or guardians who believes your child deserves the best education, support them because you never know how successful they can become. Everyone deserves a shot at following their dreams. That one goal could inspire the next generation and make a difference.

Photo Taken Of Me,
In Intensive Care
30th June, 1982.

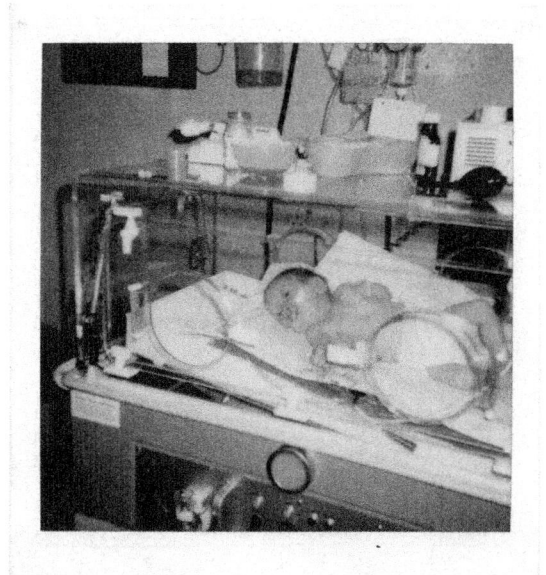

A young boy,
unaware of
what lay ahead.

A Budding Author
from A young age.

School photo with my siblings, Louis And Hollie.

My Grandmother, Maggie.

My Mum And Sister.

School photo with my six all-boy classmates

Mum, Dad, Me and With Comedian And TV Presenter Leslie Crowther.

Recieving an award from The Lovely Cheryl Baker At
The Child of Achievement Awards.

My Team At Pentwynmawr Junior Football Club.

I Was Lucky Enough To Grow Up With Great Friends.

My Dad, Brother Louis And Me On A Night Out.

I love being an uncle. Here I am with my nieces and nephews.

Newbridge Comprehensive Secondary School class photos.

Dressed as Santa at the South Wales Argus Office.

Sitting At My Desk In The South Wales Argus.

Work Colleagues
At The South
Wales Argus.

It's a Workingman I am.
I'm enjoying my job at the South Wales Argus.

CHAPTER 4
THE SPORTSMAN

"I do not have a disability, I have a gift! Others may see it as a disability, but I see it as a challenge. This challenge is a gift because I have to become stronger to get around it, and smarter to figure out how to use it; others should be so lucky."

— **Shane E. Bryan**

Growing into a teenager and finding my social identity and personality were two of the things surrounding my disabilities that my parents were most worried about. Until then, I only had one or two close family friends with whom I had interacted. But let's face it: the period of our lives where we start our teenage years is when we begin to explore and challenge new boundaries. When most of us move up to secondary school and meet new people, our social circle and hobbies expand, and teenage parties come around quickly. All the things parents hate introducing us to or even finding out about start developing: relationships, puberty, and employment further ahead. Adulthood creeps on you very quickly.

During my last year of primary school, my parents were keen to find ways to help me widen my social circle. They decided to take me to watch the martial arts club at our local community centre. My father came with me for a few sessions, and first, we only sat and watched the other children learning martial arts, which was Ki-Aikido. Surprisingly, after a few weeks of observing the Ki-Aikido class and with a bit of persuasion from the dojo's Sensei, I decided to join in.

At my first session, Sensei reassured my father that, despite my disabilities, he was confident I could participate in some exercise. Ki-Aikido would improve my quality of life, walking, and coordination. I would learn to use my body's core to improve my balance. He also told my father that getting involved would teach me about discipline and that I would make many friends. After weeks and months passed, I came to enjoy Ki-Aikido so much.

Along with starting to interact with other people other than my close family and tight-knit circle of friends, although with a high level of anxiety, I was learning social skills. These skills put me on the right path. They slowly started to bring me out of my shell and show me that there was no need to be so afraid of making new friends. Although I'm saying this, even today I still get wary when meeting or talking to someone unfamiliar, mainly because of the anxiety of thinking they may not understand what I'm saying. Admittedly, after a little while of chatting and interacting with them, people come to understand me, but it's that unknown fear of not knowing people's reactions when they hear my speech.

But starting Ki-Aikido was just the start because, from that point on, my parents were happy for me to spread my wings, explore, and start finding my way. So much so that, with specific rules, they let me play in and around the village with all the other children. As a result, my social confidence was slowly but surely growing.

BECOMING THE FOOTBALLER

Then there was this one night during the summer holidays. It was the summer before I started secondary school, and out of the blue, a family friend stopped my father and me in the street after a Ki-Aikido class and asked me if I was interested in joining the local junior football team. In the heat of this moment, I was startled. I had been offered to join an able-bodied football team. I had only just adapted to carrying out Ki-Aikido with disabilities. But Football? All that was going through my mind was that football is a contact sport. Can I play it?

Although up until this point, my parents were happy for me to get involved with Ki-Aikido classes and were happy for me to socialise by attending these classes and going out to play close to home, can I get involved with a football team comfortably? A substantial next step.

After many family discussions and being very stubborn, I begged my parents to let me at least go to a training session and see if my body was strong enough to do the basic drills. Remember. It was around a year and a half before I had learned to walk unaided, but my parents reluctantly agreed to take me to a football training session where a few of my close friends were also there.

My father had taken me shopping that morning at a sports store to kit me out with shin pads and football boots, which I wore that first training session. Still, as I walked onto the welfare ground for my first training session, there were a few laughs, and children were pointing and staring. Still, after a while, my father finally pulled me away from tightly gripping his leg after I became overwhelmed with fear and anxiety. Then, he and our family friend eventually coaxed me to join in and explained that there was no pressure on me to do any of the drills I felt my body was incapable of carrying out. After a while of joining the others in the routines and getting a feel for kicking a complete leather football, others started to stand around me, even placing the ball in front of me and encouraging me to kick it.

They began to embrace the fact that I was different, which led to a barrage of curious questions that my father and our family friend, Robin, were always on hand to help me answer. I always remember this particular moment; it was so overwhelming, but it felt like a weight had been lifted off my shoulders. I felt like somebody. I was being included and accepted by the most people I had ever met, not just by one little boy on a school playground.

As the season progressed, a special bond was starting to form between the group, and uniquely, the lads learned over time that I wasn't able to join in as much of the contact stuff as they could, and if I needed to rest and sit a session out, they'd respect that. They were growing to become protective, not only on the football field but off it. We were becoming the best of friends, a close-knit football team. We would look out for and encourage each other no matter what, and to me, this is a massive notion of inclusiveness. I felt like a part of not only a team but of the community, which was something that, until this point, I had never experienced.

Our first competitive season could have been better. We were a newly formed team finding our feet (excuse the pun). Therefore, we only won a few games, but this was our most important year because we learned so much about football and who we grew into. Amazingly, we merged into a competitive football team in the second season. We then had a few new boys join, and our already-signed lads dramatically improved our footballing abilities.

During our second preseason, we had a young lad join us. His name was Darren, and instantly, he made a massive impact on the team. From the start, we could all tell that his football skills were out of this world. He could glide past players as if they weren't even in front of him, and he could head the ball at that young age further than professional adults. When he took his first touch in training, the rest of us just stopped and looked on in amazement. We then knew we had a special player joining us.

So that second season, we all upped our game, with Darren possibly being the missing link we were looking for. From that season on, we went on to be unbeatable for the next couple of years, winning leagues and cups for fun. Darren went on to have trials for the likes of Manchester United and Nottingham Forest but could have improved his grade. He was an energetic character, always in trouble. Unfortunately, Darren is no longer with us. A few others, boys from our team, have also passed away. They are gone, but never forgotten.

The matches were great. I loved and lived for a Saturday morning. We would meet around nine o'clock for a ten-thirty kick-off. The coaches made sure all nets and flags were set up, and then we would get down to business, retreat to our changing rooms for a team talk, and get changed. The boys were great. I only had to ask if I needed help changing and lacing my boots, and they would help me.

I was forever on the bench because of my disabilities; even being involved in a matchday was special. I felt included. I didn't get on the pitch in some games because we were young. Still, we were very competitive and built a few rivalries over the years.

Still, there were games where we would completely dominate teams and score a few goals with no reply, and this is when I would get my chance to experience matchday football.

I mostly got on the field for the last ten or five minutes, enough to feel the energy and be included. There are specific memories, sights, and smells that I still remember. For example, those cold and wet winter training sessions on the local leisure centre's AstroTurf playing surface, where you would get soaked to your underwear if it was raining, arriving at our home ground on matchday on a crisp autumn Saturday morning, smelling and feeling the fresh autumn air on your face, the morning dew and fog would be lifting, and the goalpost on the far end of the football field would eventually appear from out of the depths of the mist, and then the grass would still be glistening. I used to think we were playing at the old Cardiff Arms Park instead of standing on my local council football field.

MY FOOTBALL COACH — ROBIN CHURCHILL

Nowadays, junior football is very different and has become much more professionally managed and run. Robin and I regularly reminisce about our involvement in Pentwynmawr Junior Football Club all those years ago over a beer and how happy we still are that the junior section of the club, after a few years of hiatus, is now running again with my friend Gavin Evans at the helm.

Robin now tells me how he remembers when my parents took me to my first training session, how he recalls the brilliant response from everyone who, back then, had been involved at the club, and how excited but slightly anxious and curious they were about how things would eventually unfold with a child with physical disabilities joining an able-bodied junior club. But the most pleasing thing for him, he tells me, was that the local children would never leave me out of anything—not that I would let them.

He says the teams we played against back then always wanted me on the pitch. Even though we were already fielding eleven players, they would, for a time, let us field twelve players. To this day, there are people we used to play against who still ask how I'm getting on, and they are over the moon when Robin tells them I am now an author and have written such wonderful children's books to date.

Robin has since told me that bedding me into a team of non-disabled young children took a lot of patience and determination. The under-twelve age groups and over-twelve football teams played full-pitch football, which was complete contact, and he felt a moral obligation to try and protect this little boy who was different and more vulnerable than the others. There was no turning away from this. But this was achieved by others around us being so understanding. There were many more non-disabled children playing football at the time than disabled ones, especially in the community. Disability sports teams were few and far apart then, as opposed to today.

He would ask and liaise with opposing teams before each kick-off to check if the game, weather, and field conditions were suitable and if they were happy for me to go onto the field. Even in the early days, every answer would be 'absolutely yes.' Then, as each new season went on, teams would look for me and ask if I was going to get 'my five minutes of game time.'

We would occasionally go on bonding trips or day trips. One year, we went to Nottingham to watch them play at The City Ground, and beforehand, we played their under-twelve squad as part of the trip. Even then, I was eager to get some game time.

We anticipated a more tentative reaction when Robin asked their coaching staff if they were happy for me to 'have my five minutes' of game time. But again, their response was positive, and they insisted I get on the field. We beat them eleven goals to nil with our star player, Darren, running the show. I have so many fond memories of this period of my life. The silver lining is that playing football massively contributed to my feeling accepted and finally putting to bed the fear of not fitting in.

MY JOURNEY IS A LITTLE UNIQUE!

Remember, it is okay to let yourself be accepted by others. These are my life's core values, and I take them everywhere. They are instilled in my blood. Even though my football story is unique, I wouldn't change how football is run and played nowadays from when I played. The growth of disabled football and sports teams has accelerated tremendously. I would encourage anyone with disabilities to consider getting involved in these because the social aspects benefit you from an inclusion perspective.

Being involved with my team for years has made me a better person. I don't know; I'm not an overly confident person. Still, my interaction skills are much better now that I've made so many friends because my parents encouraged me to get out into society instead of wrapping me up in cotton wool.

Contacting Disability Sport Wales is an excellent way to find out how you can get involved in a disability sports team in Wales. They are a not-for-profit organisation that is now a company limited by guarantee with charitable status. However, please be aware that if you live outside of Wales, there are many disability-minded sports organisations. You need to find the nearest one to your home and, most importantly, one that suits your child's disabilities.

DISABILITY SPORT WALES

I asked Tom Rogers, the Partnership Manager at Disability Sport Wales, how individuals are best supported to access opportunities today and how we can support disabled people to find the best options today, and he said,

"The number of opportunities for disabled children and young people is widespread across Wales and includes a wide range of sports. The primary way we support Disability Sport Wales is through the Insport programme, which supports clubs, national governing bodies of sport, local authorities, and third sector organisations to develop their inclusive provision. An example of some of these current opportunities is highlighted on our website. The following club finder will enable you to find the nearest opportunities through a postcode search."

Club finder: https://www.disabilitysportwales.com/index.php/en-gb/join-in

Further information on the Insport programme is included here: https://www.disabilitysportwales.com/index.php/en-gb/programmes/insport

When new to sport or looking for the best fit for them personally, we encourage individuals to attend an Insport Series event. A minimum of 15 are held annually, and we link these to impairment groups, local opportunities, and partners where possible. I suggest people check in here to see the latest options.
    https://www.insportseries.co.uk/

In terms of performance pathway opportunities, we manage performance pathway hubs that run across Wales, with an option for individuals (9 years old +) to signpost themselves through an inspiring form: https://www.disabilitysportwales.com/en-gb/performance/inspire-form

From June 2023, we will also have a Regional Partnership Senior Officer in post for each region of Wales who will be in post to support the respective partners to best support the development of local and regional inclusive opportunities.

Another source of some of the opportunities available can be found through our YouTube channel, including several clips put together by some of the younger pathway athletes. https://www.youtube.com/@DisabilitySportWales/featured

I hope Tom's valuable information encourages someone who picks up this book and reads it to take up disability sports wherever they live.

EVER THE SPORTSMAN

After football ended, I was still missing sports. You can't just walk away. Your competitive streak remains. By the time I finished with the junior football section after a few years of helping to coach the younger generations, I was eighteen and was now of age to serve in the local workingmen's club.

I started getting to know a few older members and have

become friends. On a Sunday, they would play a game of cards. They would play crib and don, which are typical club and pub games and are still played today.

Crib is a game that involves playing and combining cards, usually five or six. Certain combinations and tricks you use earn you points.

There are several tricks, but the main and most definitive one is scoring points for a grouping of cards that add up to fifteen. Overall, crib is a very tactical game, but you also need a lot of luck and the run of the cards. Nine cards consist of two fixed teams of two players. Don the game is point-based; each team scores points during the game, and the team with the greater total value of cards scores extra points. The first team to reach one hundred and-twenty-one wins the game.

As time passed, I started watching them play both games and eventually began to join in. My counting and mathematical qualities need to be revised to meet professorial or university standards. But the more I have played crib over the years, the more I have become pretty good at it, and since I was twenty-one, I have played in two local crib and don leagues where the team has won leagues and cups collectively. My most proud achievement is winning the county single crib competition.

Along with still playing crib and don and still trying to be good at it, my passion for sport in general is still alive, even though it's not as strong these days. Becoming an author and songwriter has grounded me, but it has been a natural progression. It has filled the void in my life after so many years of being involved with football. Everyone moves on after their sporting exploits, whether disabled or not. We don't need to let our disabilities stop us from participating in sports or games.

As I mentioned a few paragraphs ago, over the last twenty years, disability sports and their representation and coverage have progressed immensely. However, there is more to do to get anywhere near the recognition that non-disabled players are exposed to. Organisations like Disability Sport Wales and the National Lottery fund many sports and activities that are inclusive and that disabled people can get involved with. You must find one you enjoy because staying active and mobile as you age is challenging. I haven't given up just yet.

TIREDNESS AND FATIGUE

With cerebral palsy, your energy levels will vary as you go through life and get older. I know this because it happens all the time to me. I am as mobile as I can and will ever be, but in the back of my mind, I know that I have probably gone past my most active years, and generally, as we age, we become less mobile. Unfortunately, it happens to everyone, even non-disabled people. Still, we've got to come to terms with it realistically and become prepared for the fact that, with a physical disability, there's a high chance that you will become a lot less mobile a lot quicker than others.

Those of us who have cerebral palsy can become exhausted at any time, and this is due to fatigue setting in and can be overlooked and even ignored. Trust me, I know. But you have probably already sensed that I am as stubborn as they come. From my experience, it's inevitable that if you have cerebral palsy, you'll struggle with fatigue at some point. You use three to five times more energy than a non-disabled person because how your muscles behave affects how your body moves.

Our muscles go through more movements than others; sometimes, these movements can be uncontrollable, so we have spasms. Let me put this into perspective. It's like doing everything you'd typically do over three days and cramming it all into one day. It's like going to a theme park, and you rush around it so fast to get everything in and go on all the rides before it closes. Then, when you get home, you have no energy left. I'm tired just sitting here typing about it.

Think about it. People with cerebral palsy regularly burn lots of energy, so if one day they pull out of a day trip or event, this is one of the reasons why they haven't turned up. So, a little advice: please remember to be considerate if they postpone. It's nothing you've done. It can be tiring and even draining physically and mentally when you want to live life to the best of your abilities, or, in my case, with disabilities, but you can't.

From a physical perspective, my right side and my legs are affected the most. The most pain I get is in the back of my legs when my hamstrings tighten, and after walking, my legs ache. In addition, I continuously experience stiffness in my right arm, so I rarely use it. Instead, I conduct most daily chores with my left arm, which is my strongest, and then my parents always do anything strenuous or hazardous, like boiling the kettle or ironing.

It is challenging to fasten buttons on a shirt or pair of jeans. Ironing is particularly dangerous, too. My cerebral palsy affects my coordination. I could burn myself with one slip while ironing and end up with an iron pattern scorched on one of my arms, looking as if I'd just been in a comedy sketch. Finally, aside from microwavable meals, I rarely cook for myself. I live with my parents, and my mother will not let me near the kitchen, fearing I could burn the house down.

Safety is paramount. It would only be a matter of time before an accident occurred if I used a hot cooker or stove. I have smashed a few mugs, so who knows what would happen if I started carrying pans of boiling water? I'll be the first to admit that I'm a walking health and safety hazard.

RESPECTING BOUNDARIES

Growing up, I always tried to push my body to its limits. Sometimes, I forget that I am only human, not some alien species that comes from Krypton like Superman. As youngsters, we are fearless and explore danger, and I pushed myself in my younger days. I would try to run as much as other kids in the playground and dangerous areas near busy roads. But as you age, you become more aware of the dangers around you. You also realise you can put others in danger, especially with a disability like cerebral palsy where your coordination isn't as good as others, so sometimes you need to ask or rely on others for help.

Still, I also want people to understand that disabled people, like anyone else, have boundaries. They need their personal space and can ask for or accept help. However, they, too, have every right to say no. It's intuitive and part of our nature to want to assist our fellow humans if we see them struggling. Still, it's reassuring to know there are still good people in this world, because they will be the ones you find yourself turning to in your hour of need.

The crucial thing is to make sure that you are respecting the wishes of the disabled person and not overstepping their boundaries. Sadly, I've experienced the latter many times. Once, while crossing the road, a random person grabbed my arm and physically pulled me across at speed. However, that person who hadn't seen that traffic on both sides of the road acknowledged me, and I recognised and thanked them for safely letting me cross the road even before being manhandled. I didn't need their help, and apart from anything else, being randomly and unwittingly handled isn't a captivating experience, no matter how good that person's intentions are.

Because of my speech impediment, people often ask me to repeat what I'm saying if they can't understand me. For example, if the shop assistant asks me for the petrol pump number at a petrol station, I use it to get petrol. Usually, I take a step back, compose myself, try to speak more clearly, point at the pump I used, or get my communication aid app up on my phone. But, sometimes, when this happens, another person in the queue behind me impatiently shouts out the petrol pump. People are perhaps in a rush, but shouting out behind me without asking if I need help is rude and ableist.

This situation could be timely and frustrating for others, but patience and consideration as to whether or not to ask if I need help are all that's required. Don't get me wrong; it is always lovely to be offered help by a friend or someone passing by in the street. But the critical point is that the support is being offered, not just assumed. So, as much as you want to help, please take a moment to step back and ask the person if they are ok. Or can you offer any assistance? If their response is a polite 'no thank you,' they are competent in the situation or task, like putting a jacket on.

I will gladly accept your help, especially if I do something outside my capabilities, like carry a whole pint back from a bar. Hence, most of the time, I ask the bar staff to help, and 99% of the time, the person obliges because, quite frankly, if I carried it, my drink would be over the floor by the time I got to my table. But please ask if I need any help beforehand, and don't assume I am struggling because of my appearance.

So, my general advice would be that if a disabled person needs help, they'll ask. I'll only ask for help if I'm struggling to do something because I often get embarrassed when somebody takes it upon themselves to wade in and help anyway without asking. But, on the other hand, if I ask someone for help, it is because I am struggling with something, and I know it's in my best interest to get help for my safety, so the embarrassment isn't as bad.

It all comes down to risk assessment. If you see a disabled person getting along competently with something, be happy for them. Like most people, it shows their willingness to get on with their lives. Still, if they need your help, they will ask for it, so just be there when they need assistance because that's what genuine people do.

STAYING MOBILE

Around five years ago, on my thirty-sixth birthday, I noticed my legs weren't as mobile as they used to be. Let's face it. My legs have never been in top shape, and walking without taking breaks has always been challenging. Now that I'm getting into my 'golden years,' it is becoming more of a challenge. I do have cerebral palsy, after all.

I felt my hamstrings, especially my right hamstring, tighten almost continuously. I've never undergone any operations, such as a selective dorsal rhizotomy procedure when I was younger, to improve my movement. When I was young, operations like the ones I just mentioned weren't around. Even today, they are costly, with parents, family, and friends often having to fundraise to raise money to pay for the operation costs because the NHS rarely performs these procedures.

Let's talk about how my legs began deteriorating a few years ago. The COVID pandemic hadn't even hit then. I struggled to stand up for a long time, and getting up from sitting was getting more complicated. So I asked my mother to make a doctor's appointment. From there, I was referred to an orthopaedic consultant, who further referred me to the hospital for physiotherapy sessions and orthotics appointments.

I attended many physiotherapy sessions before my legs started to strengthen again. Still, in the last session, the physiotherapist sat me down and discussed how I would continue exercising to make my legs as strong as possible. They explained that staying active doesn't mean I should consider becoming Mo Farah and starting long-distance running or beginning bodybuilding and competing in 'The World's Strongest Person Competition'. Instead, it's about staying active within our capabilities.

Due to muscle reactions and stiffness, I cannot relax in a swimming pool, so this was ruled out. Also, I can't walk or run long distances, so disability or walking football wouldn't suit me. Therefore, I explained that I had always thought about joining a gym, and, to my surprise, they said, Why not? For one, a gym is somewhere you don't need to do a lot of walking. It's inclusive and community-based, where you meet new people and make friends. It's also good for your mental health.

So, I joined a gym, and within the gym I had joined, I connected with and chatted with a personal trainer, Greg Jones, who had worked with and trained people with cerebral palsy. Knowing this information and how Greg was experienced in helping people like myself who have cerebral palsy instantly put my mind at ease. The following year, leading up to the pandemic's start, I had a weekly one-on-one personal training session where we worked as a team, always mindful of my disabilities and my body's limits. We worked tirelessly on developing a simple exercise plan that concentrates on increasing my body movement without putting strain on any adverse movement in my muscles. Letting my arms and legs lead the way and not pushing my muscles in any direction they can't reach.

We worked on balance techniques, core strengthening, and positioning. Most importantly, we concentrated on training my leg muscles to be as strong as possible. Repeating these exercises over time trains your brain, which sends messages to your muscles that your legs are becoming more robust by continuously doing floor and light leg weight exercises.

So even though I'll never be able to walk as normally as other people, my overall walking is improving. I now also wear orthotic insoles. These are insoles you place into any footwear, and the heel part of the insole is a few millimetres higher than the rest, which helps to encourage your feet to step heel first and toe second. Wearing orthotic insoles has indefinitely contributed to my walking improvement. Admittedly, I sometimes still walk flat-footed, but most days, I get by, and I am now walking with my heel hitting the ground first.

The best thing about this is that I would forever drag my toes along the floor before I started wearing orthotic insoles to the gym. Meaning the front of my shoes would often have holes in them. As you can imagine, this would become costly, and I would have the extra financial burden of buying five or six pairs a year! Now, I am down to buying two pairs a year, so

I am onto a winner. Plus, my feet don't freeze, get wet, or smell so much with no holes in my shoes!

THE GYM

These days, I go to the gym once or twice a week. That's if my body fatigues; let me, and I'm not too drained. But, as I have mentioned, I always train within my body's capabilities and limits. I usually work out for around an hour for each session. During these sessions, I may get on the treadmill and, while securely holding onto the bars, do a slow walk on an incline for around two to three minutes at a time while leaning forward before resting for the same length of time, stretching my hamstrings and strengthening my calves and thighs.

Other exercises I may do are the rowing machine, ski-erg machine, and some loose, light upper body weight training routines, allowing my arms and muscles to go in the direction they need or want to go at all times; floor work; and exercises using different weighted medicine balls; this is good for your core and balance. In addition, I may go on the pulldown bar weights to improve my upward reach and shoulder movement, and I often go on the leg press and calf extension weight machines to further strengthen these areas. But, again, I always exercise within my limits and capability-assessed distances so as not to pull any muscles or hurt myself.

GREG JONES - PERSONAL TRAINER

"Gavin contacted me via Facebook, asking if I could work with him as his personal trainer. He explained his physical limitations, and we arranged to meet at the gym to discuss working together and what we could achieve.

In the meeting, Gavin arrived with a note explaining his condition. He wasn't the first client I had worked with who had cerebral palsy, but his condition was far more limiting than my previous client's, and Gavin's verbal constraints were also new to me. It was a real eye-opener for me to have chatted with Gavin over a message to meet him then and try to communicate.

I knew it would be a real challenge to safely discover Gavin's physical limits without causing harm and to communicate with each other effectively. On reflection, after our first meeting, the challenge that I faced was nothing compared to the one Gavin would be facing, and I found myself excited by the journey we would be taking. Unlike so many of my clients in the past who had significant weight loss goals or sporting events to prepare for, Gavin's goals were much more down-to-earth. He was looking to become more mobile and keep his range of motion without dragging his foot and tearing a hole in his new trainers.

I had already done a lot of research into the physical challenges that cerebral palsy brings. For example, a lot of medical science discourages physical exertion. Still, several men and women on social media have disproved this, so Gavin and I knuckled down and explored what his body had to offer. We carefully tracked every training session, logging the weights, small steps, and limited distances Gavin achieved. In addition, Gavin would provide me with feedback on how his body felt in the days following our sessions. Gavin quickly grew in confidence and started attending the gym outside of our sessions, implementing our established work and allowing me to push him harder in each personal training session.

Communication became no issue; we quickly understood each other, and the sessions flowed. Gavin's progress was beyond anything I had expected, and a few months later, I had a photo from Gavin of his nice white shiny daps, and his white trainers looked like they had just come out of the box!

Gavin eventually became independent of me, carrying on with his routines and working himself into a bath of sweat in my gym! The time I spent with Gavin changed me as a personal trainer and as a person. I wasn't aware of the discrimination I had pre-programmed into me before I met Gavin. I assumed a person as nonverbal as Gavin would not be as funny, intelligent, ambitious, and talented as he was. I opened my eyes and have become more conscious of not making assumptions about people. Gavin inspired me to be a better person, and whenever I have felt under pressure or defeated by a task, I remind myself of the strength, grit, and determination Gavin shows daily and pushes through."

Greg Jones, CEO & Personal Trainer of Evolution Fitness

. . .

Remember, this is my unique mobility story. All disabilities are different, and our bodies' limitations vary massively. I value and respect that fact. I am as mobile as I will ever get, and I am mindful that I am incredibly blessed to be able to get around for now. There are people out there who are completely immobile, and I respect every disabled person out there emotionally and physically.

Remember, we are all special and unique in our own way. I'm as mobile as my body allows and know that my circumstances could change and worsen at any moment. I accept this, mentally and physically. In the past, I have struggled to come to terms with my physical appearance. Now, I am managing my mobility to the point that I've somewhat found a place where I am beginning to accept my disabilities after quite some time. Still, I am not in a position where I love my body's appearance, but I'll continue to work on myself.

My balance and walking techniques are still fragile. But, without seeking medical help a few years ago, I would probably be a lot worse than I currently am.

Lastly, I want to emphasise the importance of seeking professional and medical help before undertaking any physical activity. If you believe your quality of life could improve with exercise, always consult your doctor before taking these steps. When you have cerebral palsy, your muscles behave differently from others. Therefore, patience and slowness when using them during exercise are paramount. It will help if you are shown how to always exercise correctly.

Parents sometimes want their children to reach for the top and possibly become sporting superstars if they are talented and sporty. But the truth is that only a handful of people become creditable and successful sports stars. For example, I have often wondered if I would have ever played rugby for Wales or football for Manchester United if I were non-disabled. There's a truthful and well-used saying, 'It's the taking part that counts.'

Becoming part of a community football team helped me in many ways. It made me feel accepted and allowed me to build relationships with many people. It also furthered my independence and built my confidence to interact in public. As a result, it has improved my quality of life.

Of course, you could say that my parents letting me join a non-disabled sports team was risky, and I could have seriously injured myself. Still, as a teenager, you are much less aware of those risks, both physically and mentally. I have no regrets about how my football days went, and I am glad my parents took that risk all those years ago.

These days, the sporting world is very different, with more emphasis on risk assessment, health and safety, and even the importance of safeguarding people's mental health. Still, suppose you put me in the shoes of parents today whose disabled children are interested in playing sports at whatever level. In that case, I want to encourage them to explore every option that allows their children to fulfil their sporting aspirations, especially with the acceleration of disability sports today, like the Paralympics, because of interaction, inclusiveness, breaking down barriers, and achieving goals. It could change a disabled child's outlook on life, improve their social skills, inspire the next generation of disabled sports stars, and challenge diverse stereotypes, enabling disabled sports to become more represented, visible, and even professional in the years ahead. Ultimately, the final decision on whether they want to pursue disability sports lies with the disabled child or person. The only person who knows your body's limits is yourself.

CHAPTER 5
THE WORKINGMAN

"When you focus on someone's disability you'll overlook their abilities, beauty and uniqueness. Once you learn to accept and love them for who they are, you subconsciously learn to love yourself unconditionally." — **Yvonne Pierre**,

As previously mentioned, secondary school was the furthest I would go regarding my education. Once I had sat my exams, that was the final time I was granted funds for one-to-one support, and to tell the truth, losing this support scared me. You can imagine going from having a continuous and strong support network around you almost all the time during school hours to completely nothing. It was like having my arms ripped off. It was as if the whole world had caved in on me.

I also had the added worry of waiting for my exam results, and I now know that not getting the grades I dreamed of achieving wasn't the end of the world. Revision wasn't my strong point; I blagged most of my exams and hoped for the best. I sat most of them in a separate room from everyone else in the main school hall, under a teacher's supervision at all times. I was allowed to ask my nursery nurse to help me do certain things, like underlining words or holding my exam paper down while I wrote my answers to the exam questions. Although having someone watch me sit my exams in a one-on-one situation was strange, to some extent, I felt imprisoned and under a little more pressure than the others in the main hall.

Still, I did the best I could. It was like I was in detention or the 'naughty boy's' corner. Sitting my exams away from the others felt surreal, which, if I weren't disabled, wouldn't have happened. I would have sat in the main hall in a line of exam desks, and I know this sounds stupid. I wish I had done this because I would have felt more included.

Thinking back to my school years, especially when I knew I needed to try and revise for an exam, a sense of pointless dread would come over me. I knew what would come: sitting for an exam in a lonely room because I was different and needed assistance. Before I even picked up a book, I was subconsciously treated differently from the other pupils. Mentally, it put me at a disadvantage to others, and sitting exams after the exam was exhausting, which hindered my preparation before and during them. Besides, I had too much fun partying to find time to revise. I was still coming to terms with losing my support and rebelling, and forgetting about what lay ahead for a summer, or even a little longer, was how I consciously dealt with this.

COLLEGE

The summer had come and gone, the new college term had already started, and I was still in a rebellious mood. I remember my parents persuading me to enrol in an open learning centre on an old, shut-down South Wales Colliery site to participate in a computer skills course. Still, I only attended briefly due to what they were teaching. I had studied GCSE information technology anyway and needed to progress. However, I was willing to give college a try.

My parents even asked the college to enrol me late, and I agreed to join the AS Information Technology Course. So, I went to college, just like any other student, alone. Remember, I had no one-on-one support, and from my parent's perspective, they were looking ahead, and they knew it was time for me to stand on my own two feet.

The first morning, I caught the service bus to college and had my rucksack with everything I needed: pens, pencils, notepads, and all the usual college things.

Some of my old school friends were studying the same course and had given me all the material and notes I needed to catch up on what they had already learned in previous lectures. I turned up at the college reception and showed the lady my enrolment letter. The lady then gave me directions to the information technology block, and I made my way to the classroom, where some of my friends were already there and settled in. They had already bonded with everyone else on the course, so they were all getting along. I then found a seat and nervously prepared for the lesson, which was a strange moment because my nursery nurse at school would assist me with setting up classes before this.

I felt anxious, and immediately, my concentration fell. It was like I was entering a realm I had never experienced before. I wanted to break down and disappear into thin air, but somehow I held it together for that hour-long lecture. I never wrote a word or made a note. It was like I was in a time-lapse. My anxiety was through the roof, and I didn't want anyone to feel it was sky-high.

At the end of my first and only college lecture, I repacked my bag as quickly and best I could, didn't say a word to anybody, made my way to the college's main exit doors, and then saw the bus for home was at the bus stop, stepped on it, and made my way home. Only to cry to my mother, hoping my anxiety would go away.

I was adamant I wasn't going to attend college again, and in my heart, I knew deep down, probably from the minute I left school, that college wasn't for me. Still, my parents didn't want me to stay stagnant or get left behind. They knew that the only way for me to gain life experience and to show people that even with disabilities, there's a role for everyone within society, even if we are not as academically gifted as others.

I NEEDED A JOB

Ironically, I started to buy the local newspaper. I would go to the newsagents every Thursday and buy the local newspaper because Thursday was 'job advertisement day'. I would apply for administration or typist jobs for the following weeks and months. I even applied for apprenticeships with well-known companies but needed luck.

Maybe my disabilities had a part to play back then, and the unknown pressures or weaknesses of employing a disabled person played a role. It was and still is challenging for employers to take on disabled people, and hopefully, these attitudes will change.

The Welsh Government now has responsibility for employment and skills, while the UK Government is still in charge of employment support and social security, according to research that Claire Thomas and Joe Wilks compiled and published in an article on the Research Senedd Wales website on April 27, 2023. Claire and Joe's findings claim that in 2022, the UK government will have hit its goal of seeing a million more disabled people at work, but this only tells part of the story. While more disabled people work, the gap between working-age disabled and non-disabled people has increased.

The campaign group Disability Rights UK continues to argue that barriers to disabled people getting employment do not lie with disabled people but with society, including inaccessible transport, poor employer attitudes, inadequate flexible working, and access to the workplace that fails to make reasonable adjustments.

By May 2022, a million more disabled people would be at work. However, data for July to September shows the disability employment rate has fallen since the same time last year, with the non-disabled employment rate rising. This means the disability employment gap (i.e., the gap between working-age disabled and non-disabled people) was at its widest since 2018. Currently, at 32.3 percentage points, the disability employment gap here in Wales is higher than in the UK (29.8 percentage points).

THE SOUTH WALES ARGUS

Back in 1999, one Thursday evening, my father was reading our local newspaper, particularly the 'job advertisement section'. Our local newspaper was looking for a part-time typist (was this fate?). So, like the previous million job posts, I sent in my cover letter and a CV, and to my excitement and surprise, I got invited for an interview for this job. My father drove me to the local newspaper offices, where he accompanied me in my interview to help with any initial communication issues. This was my first interview, and with all the career advice lessons and CV writing practice I had previously learned, this was it. It was all or nothing.

I was shaking like a leaf throughout the interview, along with my habit of overthinking again. My internal ableism turned up to the maximum, and I thought my speech would put me at an instant disadvantage again, but the interview went well. The person interviewing me understood every word I said or acted as they did. After the interview, I had shaken the interviewer's hand and got home. I was genuinely happy with how my first interview went. The interview gave me a lot of confidence, and I was content that I had managed to get through the whole interview and gained invaluable experience, even if it meant never getting a job.

Still, this wasn't the last I heard from the local newspaper because two days after the interview, my father received a phone call saying they were happy to offer me the role of a part-time typist with an initial three-month probation period 'because of the unknown consequences of not being entirely sure I could cope in an office environment.' I was the best candidate they had interviewed. I will never forget when Dad told me I had secured my first job. I was breaking down barriers. I was staring my worst fears and anxieties straight in the eye. Finally, finally, I was becoming a man.

Working for the newspaper played an integral role in my transition into adulthood. I suppose it pushed me to grow up quickly, a lot quicker than I would have if I had gone to college, and being different and having disabilities was a blessing in disguise. Also, being around and working with experienced professionals from the start gave me a sense of direction. Yes, I did need extra help in and around the office, but it wasn't the one-on-one support I had previously. Someone was always on hand if I needed help, and the transition from full-on support to having so many wonderful colleagues who supported me when I needed it was and has been the perfect fit for me. It was a transition that felt so natural. It allowed me to manage the anxiety of stepping out into the world without the full support I had always been used to and without facing so many different hurdles, like preparing for numerous different subjects and lectures. The hurdles scared me.

Nowadays, I can resonate with other disabled workers, fears of negative judgement and how they could affect you in your role. Throughout this book, I talk about 'overthinking' from my perspective. I always overthink, especially in bed. One of the things overthinking drives and leads to is anxiety. You play things out in your mind; this happened when I started work, and undoubtedly, other disabled people have done so.

For example, you wonder if you could be seen as inferior or if your academic or skill-set abilities could be underestimated or scrutinised more than other colleagues. You also worry about things like progression in your job. Will your disabilities hinder situations like workload appraisals, and if so, could they end up stopping you from being considered for promotions or highly pressured managerial roles? Looking back, I could have communicated more. My attitude for many years was to get to work, work, get through the day at all costs, and earn your crust.

I sometimes overworked to try and type as fast as possible to impress. Still, this was my way of keeping up with the rest of my colleagues, and being as functional as them in a workload capacity would be sufficient for me to stay in my role. Unfortunately, by doing this and possibly not speaking up and asking if

I could have extra rest time, I would regularly get blisters on my wrist. I'm not too fond of the feel of wrist rests, so I periodically wore sweatbands to the office while using the keyboard mostly all day, pulling them over my wrists. But blisters still occurred.

Still, my stubbornness and determination drove me on, at least for seventeen and a half years. At least I can take extended breaks while writing this memoir, and it's way more enjoyable. I once read a quote by Bill Gates, the founder of Microsoft: 'I choose a lazy person to do a hard job. Because a lazy person will find an easy way to do it.' Knowing this, I could be a lot more lazy. At least whatever I'm working on, I'll be able to find the simplest and quickest way to finish the job instead of doing it the hard way.

ACCESSIBILITY IN THE WORKPLACE

Another fear or barrier that disabled employees face is the lack of accessibility in and around workplaces. Many of our new office buildings nowadays are built by contracted building companies that aren't disability awareness-savvy due to a lack of disability awareness and accessibility knowledge. There are things such as disability aids and tools that employers and building contractors forget to consider or implement that are vital to disabled people's work lives, like wheelchair ramps, accessible restrooms and toilets, automatic doors, and assistive technologies like accessible websites with digital accessibility features for people with visual and mobility issues.

From a personal perspective, I coped well in an office environment, although no provisions were in place for a disabled employee. For example, I was eventually given my disability parking space. However, sometimes, when I arrived for work, someone took my parking space, and I ended up in a non-accessible parking space. Also, there weren't any ramps, automatic doors, or ramps in most places, and for some strange reason, there wasn't an accessible toilet inside the office. There was one for customers in the reception area, which meant I needed to step outside the office every time I needed the toilet, wading through queues and groups of clients or customers making inquiries at the reception desk. Where's the logic, accessibility, personal space, decency, and privacy in all of that?

I was an employee who worked in the office for long hours, not an infrequent visitor. Still, I could get around, just about, but thinking back If I were a wheelchair user, I probably would have struggled.

IMPOSTER SYNDROME

I was made redundant from my role at the newspaper at the end of 2015, and it was one of the most horrible periods of my adult life. Over many years of working for the newspaper, redundancies occurred numerous times. Experiencing and going through multiple redundancy consulting periods was physically and even more mentally exhausting. Not knowing whether it's your turn for 'the chop' or whether you'll be losing lifelong work colleagues and friends is heartbreaking.

Then there are the many rumours that fly around the office, like a game of Chinese whispers but on a larger scale, and I still hold onto the dread feeling when I hear these rumours about 'who's going' and 'who's staying'. Contributing to more anxiety and internal ableism you experience when at work, always wondering if your disabilities will ultimately put you on top of the 'chop list' because there are plenty more employees around you who are more able and are a more secure and safe asset to the company moving forward. These feelings did contribute to me becoming stressed at times. Still, I kept myself in 'autopilot mode' and kept going right until the end and until it was my turn for 'the chop'.

These feelings of dread, anxiety, and 'self-worthlessness' crept back into my life for a long time after I had 'the chop'. To some extent, I then blamed and questioned myself and my ability to work because of my disabilities. My imposter syndrome soared to the max, and I would retreat to overthinking again for some time after, wondering if I would ever be capable enough to work again.

After I was made redundant, I went into a shell. I was embarrassed about being out of work. I felt empty, almost sick. I was so worried about how I was going to survive. Until now, I had always worked, receiving only benefits that support people with long-term disabilities for help getting around with a disability that wasn't nearly enough to live on.

FACING UP TO MY PAST

It was a long time after I had finished work when my rock of a mother dragged me to the Citizens Advice Bureau, where I got the help I needed. Before and during this time, I stupidly decided to subconsciously erase all the good times I had working with my ex-colleagues and friends because I was so embarrassed. But it wasn't until a long time after this that the embarrassment started to fade—not until I bumped into a former work colleague in a situation where I had to interact with them. To my surprise, it was just as if we were still working together, but we were reconnecting again after a long time.

I will not name this person in this book for anonymity reasons, and I have given them my word. Due to this agreement, this person has agreed to contribute to this book by sharing their perspective through their own eyes on how they saw me as one of their colleagues and explaining how they felt I was treated as a disabled worker at the place where we worked.

ANONYMOUS PERSON

"It wasn't till I sat down and recalled how awful the company was at the time and how unsupportive some people were. It upsets me to think of how things were. I wish I had been far more outspoken. In saying that, I'm so incredibly glad Gavin was welcomed and loved by so many people and that the positives—the genuinely friendly and good people—far outweighed the ableist sceptics.

There is so much about that place that is wrong. You don't realise how bad it was until you are gone. I don't even know how I feel about the place. I have sadness, anger, and embarrassment all floating around in my head. There were some good moments, too.

Disability awareness wasn't something we dealt with regularly at work. After all, we had no 'real disabilities' in the workforce. There was occasionally someone with hearing difficulties or vision impairment, but no one who was less mobile or had additional needs. As an office, we were a 1960s two-story building with no fundamental provisions for anyone with movement restrictions. Even visitors who were wheelchair-bound couldn't easily enter the building as there was no dropped kerb, the front door couldn't be opened from a wheelchair, and the main office area had a step up to it and more inaccessible doors. The second floor had no lift and was entirely unsuitable for anyone with disabilities. In today's terms, it was a health and safety nightmare.

When we first heard that a 'disabled person' was coming in for an interview, there was a sudden panic. There were a million questions around the building that had never been asked before, from disabled parking, office access, accessible toilets, ramps, accessible desks, special equipment, emergency procedures—the list was endless. There were one or two voices who believed that there was little point in interviewing someone with disabilities anyway, as they were never going to be able to work in the department.

Gavin was interviewed for a position in our advertising production department. I want to remember what encompassing title the department had at the time, as it went through a series of names over the years. The roles were mostly for computer designers who were creative. There were a few administrative roles in the department, too. Some wrongly assumed that Gavin would only be capable of performing one of the administrative jobs in the corner away from the 'main action.' However, Gavin could do far more than many had anticipated.

We soon learned he had cerebral palsy, speech issues, and restricted movement issues. This was all new territory for us. We had no previous experience with users who needed additional equipment. As it turned out, Gavin was one of the least problematic people we had and needed very little extra equipment aside from a slightly more sophisticated chair and a wristrest. Everything else was the same as everyone else's. Gavin worked on producing ads with ease and, apart from being unable to use the telephone, operated mainly in the same way as everyone else.

Gavin eventually had a parking space at the front of the building, but another employee frequently used it in order to avoid walking from the main parking lot. The rest of the building remained as it was. The only accessible toilet was in the reception area, which was back through a security door and down a step. Gavin managed to change the perceptions of the few who believed that employing someone with disabilities was a token gesture. Those who had doubted that the decision to hire someone with disabilities was proved well and truly wrong as Gavin showed that he was an asset to the company."

PURSUE YOUR DREAMS

Despite my employment experiences, my advice for career-driven disabled people is: if you want to work, go for it! The hardest part is overcoming a negative mindset caused by stagnant ableist attitudes and barriers. Never give up on job opportunities. Pursue them, and keep knocking on doors until one eventually opens. Don't take no for an answer.

If you have the attributes and talent to perform an employment role, they will outshine your disabilities, trust me. Once your foot is in that door, cooperate, do any potential probation period to the best of your abilities, show them your worth, and prove to them that they were right to employ a disabled person. Please avoid falling into the same trap as I did by not speaking up more about your emotional and physical needs and requirements to enable you to carry out your work. Looking back, I was reluctant, and I would say now frightened, to ask or complain about the lack of access or any workspace provisions I needed because I was scared that it would go against me, putting my bosses in an awkward situation, thinking they would have the power within their budgets to allow the office space around me to be made more accessible.

"In my mind, I would think, Gavin, struggle on." There's no need to cause a fuss, which could lead to me losing the job I had worked so hard to get.

Research your disabled employment rights and what they protect you for in this day and age, and keep on top of them because legislation changes all the time. I now wish I had when I was employed. Never be afraid to stand up for your rights, and always strive to break down barriers by possibly advising your employers on how they can make their company inclusive and accessible. They could be the ones who become world leaders and lead the way in disability employment for future generations. Reach for the stars, but never compromise your health and well-being by overdoing anything. If you are struggling with your workload, speak out.

Still, an office-based environment gave me a routine; within this routine, I learned the skills I need to get by as a disabled person today, like time-keeping and organisational skills, how to work to tight deadlines, and most importantly, social skills. During my seventeen years—yes, seventeen years—working at the newspaper, I made so many friends and will never forget this part of my life. I started as a typist and then learned on the job, slowly moving on to working with property database input and template makeup and taking on a similar role with editorial templates.

DISCOVERING MY PASSION

The last few years of working in an office environment were torn. Sometimes, I loved working in an office, and working for a newspaper is a role that I will always cherish; but when I was made redundant, my passion for writing grew. All I wanted to do was write songs and books. My desire to pursue an unknown direction and become a published author increased.

But as an overthinker and worrier, my internal ableism kept me wondering. Would people see me as a failure? Would people know that I wanted to write more to try and make a difference for the generations of disabled people, to inspire, and to try and change societal attitudes that being accepted for who you are is ok? My biggest fear after finishing employment was, 'would I be scorned for getting disability benefits?'

I am a very proud person. I am so proud to be Welsh. Life evolves, and I hate being stagnant, for those who know me well. My expectations are high, and my desire to do my best in everything I put my hands to is sky high, and I always try. Unfortunately, sometimes I try too much and forget about the more essential necessities in life, such as personal care, well-being, mental health, and happiness. You can get so wrapped up in trying to 'keep up' with or even 'out-stage' others.

FINDING THE COURAGE TO ASK FOR HELP

I was practically a teenager when I landed the job at my local newspaper, and then, for the next seventeen or so years, I worked and earned to live and to make ends meet. But when this stops, the realisation and fear hit, your pride takes a beating, and the thought of applying for more disability benefits up until this point scared me. Even though my family and friends tried to reassure me that I was entitled to benefits as much as anyone with disabilities and wouldn't be frowned upon for getting help, my stubborn conscience told me the opposite. It wasn't until quite some time after I had left the newspaper that my mother persuaded me to seek advice from the Citizens Advice Bureau.

"How are you going to be able to get the care you need? How are you going to be able to survive financially?" My mother would hastily shout and try to break through my stubborn pride.

I still remember my first Citizens Advice meeting being at our local church. I was waiting to be called into a room at the back of the church to discuss my options with a lady I didn't even know. I was at my lowest. I was embarrassed, but my mother was right by my side, as she always has been—my rock. It's fair to say now. If my mother hadn't marched me into that church, I probably would have never been here writing this book, and you wouldn't be reading it.

That particular meeting shaped my life. It meant I could

see that my stubbornness to let go of my stupid pride was uncalled for, even though, at this point, **I was still nowhere near ready to step on the long road to begin trying to accept my disabilities.** I still refused to accept my disabilities. The lady at Citizen Advice explained step-by-step that having disabilities and the associated benefits are means-tested, and it was in my best interest to get them. Receiving disability benefits doesn't mean you are failing. It's entirely the opposite and has nothing to do with being employed or unemployed because they are designed to help with essential everyday responsibilities that we, as disabled people, may need extra help with, like getting around and those essential care duties we may need or want.

You can even do some voluntary, permitted work or earn so much a week before you need to chat with the Department of Work and Pensions about possible benefit changes while getting disability benefits, which others sometimes don't realise. I now know that back then, refusing to get help was not necessary. There was no need to get embarrassed, refuse to let my pride take a knock, or even worry about what other people who don't know how the welfare system for seriously disabled people works think. Disability benefits are to help people like me get around, go to hospital appointments, go shopping, and do everyday chores like non-disabled people. I advise disabled people and parents of disabled children who are a little anxious about finding out about or applying for help because they are worried about being seen as pocket-pinching and being frowned upon to please don't be embarrassed to ask for help because these benefits help us to live every day for the better.

REFLECTING

If I had gone to college and university, I might have learned and developed different life skills and a little more independence. But thus far, I have coped with support from family and friends. Everyone is different in many ways, too. Remember, our disabilities, or even our abilities, only make up a small part of us, and many disabilities exist.

Some are physical. Some have hidden disabilities. Other people have learning disabilities, and others suffer from mental health problems. Still, we all have a right to education or to pursue a professional or working career.

Others are more academically talented than others. Some people are more creative. Some are sportier and more gifted than others. We all have the right to not only follow our dreams but to help others realise theirs and enable them to have a shot at success.

Some may accomplish great things. Others may not. Always being you, believing in yourself, and doing something to your best ability is all that matters. Do what makes you happy. If my parents hadn't fought for me to attend mainstream education, my life could be very different now, and I wouldn't be where I am today.

MY ADVICE ON PURSUING TALENT

My advice for young parents with children with disabilities is to believe in them, see that they have a unique talent, fight for them, support them, and don't be afraid of letting them fly. Remember, the societal attitudes and barriers around us halt us, not always our disabilities.

My life has changed a lot since I finished work. It has changed completely, and for the better. I'm a lot happier now. Looking back, being made redundant in December of 2015 wasn't the best Christmas present I have received, but it was a blessing in disguise and was the push I needed to break away from the awful circus theatre of employment I was essentially in. I was a guinea pig, a 'see how it goes' employee, and an experiment that a few ableist and uneducated people wanted to brush under the carpet from the moment I stepped into my interview, all because of fear and the lack of disability employment awareness there was and still is.

I am now pursuing and living my lifelong dream of being a writer. Admittedly, financially, the life I have now, stability-wise, is a world away from when I had a full-time job. Still, money isn't everything, and having that worrying feeling from month to month about whether I will make ends meet does keep me on my toes. It comes with the territory of being disabled and a freelance writer, I guess. Still, the fact that I am making a difference to others by finally following my heart and dreams and showing that even though disabled people may navigate their careers differently, we can still achieve incredible things now firmly puts me in a position where I can put the views of those few 'ex-employer sceptics' in the past, feeling no shame towards that period of my life, and even though I still sometimes experience imposter syndrome.

I know I have only good people around me, like my family, friends, and supporters. There's no shying away from the fact that my career change has been highly challenging, and I wouldn't change it for the world. But one of the key positives about becoming a disabled writer is that I am more visible within society, and this is how I can continue to become part of a unique group of people who lead the way by advocating for a more inclusive and diverse society for all disabled people by attending numerous events like networking, music industry gigs, sometimes public speaking, and many author events.

MEETING NEW PEOPLE AND HEARING THEIR STORIES

Along the way, I get to talk to many people from all walks of life. Not everyone I meet is disabled or is from the same background as I am. Still, being a writer doesn't mean that I am tied to an office like when I was at the newspaper, which is great; it's a whole new world to me and can sometimes be very difficult because of my speech. I am now meeting many exciting new and different people, striking up those interesting and awkward conversations about disability.

It's not as if I can avoid having these kinds of conversations the way I do. Still, as I've mentioned before, talking about our disabilities helps educate others, and sometimes, as much as these conversations can be awkward and even intrusive, it is fine with me. So much so that I was not long ago at a disability awareness event with my book publisher, where we met someone and incidentally started chatting about our past disability employment experiences. Even though this person wasn't disabled and had worked in the performing arts theatre sector, the similarity in terms of a lack of compassion and disability awareness from a well-being, health and safety, and accessibility perspective by an employer was startling.

To recently find this out about modern-day employers, companies, and especially our public sector employers, who deal with disabled people from all walks of life daily, is highly worrying and raises the question of whether the government, for one, is taking the lives and well-being of disabled employees seriously and whether employers are still fearful of taking on disabled people because they don't have the correct practices and legalisations in place. It seems to me that even though we are now in 2023, the fear factor of employing disabled workers and adapting to their needs is still revered and brushed under the carpet, just like I was at the newspaper years ago.

It was fascinating sitting down and speaking to this person. It was as if I were unexpectedly transported back to my working days and reliving my working nightmare and outdated ableist attitudes. I had to stop myself from becoming angry and embarrassed again. I held those imposter syndrome feelings back, preventing specific bad memories from those days from flooding back to me. This person went on to tell me that they would be more than happy to share their story in this book, and this is what they said:

ANONYMOUS WHISTLEBLOWER

"I want to shout about it. Funnily enough, I have just received my employment tribunal letter, which is scary; however, I am ready for battle. This situation is not about winning for me; this is all about and has always been about why I raised profound disability awareness, health and safety, and fire safety concerns, and I was telling the truth. Instead of my employer putting these basic practices in place and being honest, it wasn't being done, maybe subjecting management to disciplinary action. They have backed them and subjected me to treatment I couldn't take anymore, and I forced myself to resign from a twenty-year job.

I raised the following issues with my employer informally: whistleblowing and a formal grievance. There were no fire drills at the three theatres during my employment. Risk assessments need to be more current or updated. We have evacuation chairs, but no one is trained to use them. Disabled and wheelchair users are not considered in the evacuation plan. Only take them to the refuge point. At two of our theatres, wheelchair users use the lift to get to their seats or spaces. What happens when there is an evacuation or lift breakdown? How do we get these people out?

As the duty supervisor, whose role is to take the lead in evacuating the three theatres, I last received any fire safety training in 2015. I felt morally obligated to raise these kinds of essential issues. It was my job. Every shift, I had to fill out a show report. Many times, I would raise these concerns via this reporting system. It was my job to take a lead role in an evacuation as the duty supervisor, and I needed to be more confident that the staff would be able to assist me in an evacuation or lift breakdown.

It was not received as positively as intended whenever I raised a concern. It was often stated that this differed from your role's remit. I argued this point and said I oversaw that shift, so it was my job because you, as my employer, expect me to do everything in my job profile.

I decided management was not taking these informal concerns seriously, so I whistled blew in the public's interest and filed a formal grievance as an employee. I raised the following: There are no fire drills in any of our three venues. Means of escape for the disabled user, including wheelchairs. Radio communication is not sufficient and needs to be fixed. Risk assessments and a lack of training need to be updated.

I asked that they visit all sites and view all documentation and legislation. The local council chose only to visit two venues. They made recommendations to management, and the whistleblowing case was closed. The venue they decided not to see was because someone had undertaken the visits before leaving the authority. They were satisfied that the visits to the two venues demonstrated that management arrangements were in place. As the same management arrangements are applied across the three venues, there was no requirement to visit the third venue.

This venue's lift, the only means of escape for wheelchair users, has been highlighted as non-compliant with the most basic DDA requirements, and they chose not to visit this venue.

I can only comment from my experience on how this affected me when the correct legal accessibility, health and safety, and fire regulations weren't in place. Mentally, it was draining and a constant battle to be heard and for it to be taken as it was intended. To get better and understand what they, as an employer, must do. It was stressful having that responsibility in my role and praying every shift that nothing happened, knowing that if it did, we couldn't get these people out. I am proud of myself for speaking up about the failures within the organisation I worked for. However, I needed help to fight a public venue the council ran alone. My health declined, and it is still clear that they are not taking this seriously.

Instead of taking my complaints as intended and fixing them, they are spending valuable time and public money to find me the unreasonable one. I no longer wanted to be part of that culture and was forced to resign after a twenty-year career.

I have no regrets, except one: I should have whistle blown to the disabled community rather than my employer."

CHAPTER 6
THE SONGWRITER

"I was slightly brain damaged at birth, and I want people like me to see that they shouldn't let a disability get in the way. I want to raise awareness – I want to turn my disability into ability." —**Susan Boyle**

Up until age fifteen, I was still involved with my village football team. I loved every minute. But, although I knew the time would come as my friends and I were growing up, I didn't want to believe that they would progress to youth and senior football without me. Honestly, this was one of the hardest decisions I have had to make. Seeing all my friends move on to youth and senior football without me was horrible.

I'm the first to admit I'd never be the next George Best. His balance while dribbling past opposing players on a football field was far superior to mine. With one strong gust of wind, I'm stumbling, turning, and performing cartwheels faster than a gymnast can, despite trying to control a football with these two left feet. With my friends moving on, I had to agree that I would never be involved with football again.

However, I was thankfully asked to become part of the coaching setup for one of the up-and-coming junior teams, a role I enjoyed. It removed the hard blow I had encountered previously by hanging my boots up. I was involved with guiding the youngsters to successive league and cup titles over the next few years, and it was a role I put everything into. But, even then, there came a time when the boys I was coaching were moving on, and the reality hit home. My overall involvement with the football team was over.

FINDING MYSELF THROUGH MUSIC

Being a typical teenager, I became a little rebellious for the next four years. I partied and started going out to music gigs and nightclubs. It was as if the music soothed the blow of not being involved with football. I began to fall in love with music.

I had always loved to write, as I mentioned about enjoying writing in my school years, and up until this point, I hadn't written anything for many a year because of playing football and partying like George Best (let's face it though, George was a lot better looking than me and could pull off the party animal lifestyle a lot better). Something was missing in my life, and I had no direction except working for the newspaper, which eventually took up a large chunk of my life for seventeen years.

Around the time I started working, my parents' relationship wasn't great, and things weren't going well for them for a while, resulting in their splitting. The end of my parents' marriage left me with several unanswered questions, like, 'were the years prior as a tight family unit fighting many ableist barriers because of my disabilities and the stress a contributing factor to their breakup?' Then I wondered if I would eventually end up living alone while getting care when they would ultimately find new love and lives. Remember, back then, I was still pretty young and had only lived with and been cared for by my parents. Even then, I knew disabled adults being cared for by personal assistants always happened.

The thought of facing new fights or barriers alone and not with the family I had always been used to and felt safe living with, thinking about the prospect of being cared for by strangers, scared me. Still, things eventually worked out, and since my parents split, I have lived with my mother and now with her and her new husband for the past nine years, and they haven't managed to get rid of me yet. It will take a strong woman to persuade me to leave home. Still, stranger things have happened.

At the time, I was still in my youthful rebellious mode, sometimes partying until the early hours, on weeknights too, then getting my head down for a couple of hours at best before heading to work and sometimes working nine, ten, or anything up to fourteen-hour shifts due to extra supplement newspaper titles being printed some weeks. It got pretty wild sometimes. Even with cerebral palsy, when my legs would be aching, I stayed on autopilot. I stupidly worked to party, then lived within my means afterwards, often exceeding them.

SONGWRITING BECAME MY THERAPY

I began to write again to deal with the aftermath and dismay of my parents' separation. I had never told anyone how much my parents' separation had affected me. My creative flair started to reignite; it became a way to channel my thoughts and feelings—a natural therapy. I was effectively using writing as a counselling process, helping me to chase the sadness of this enormous change in my life out of me.

Anyone who has gone through the agony of their parents splitting up knows how tough witnessing the process is. At this particular time, your emotions run high, and it isn't until some time after you sit back and evaluate why people break up and their reasoning for doing so that things go wrong, but essentially, we all have the right to choose our destiny and be happy. You will better understand how and why as you get older and wiser. I believe experiencing this has consciously played a significant part in why I started to write lyrics: to chase the dismay and that youthful party animal out of me and stay focused on making a difference and being a visible advocate for the disabled community.

I studied song structures, rhythm, form, rhyme, and syllables. I was so determined to focus on my newly reconciled passion for writing that I wrote nearly every day for a good year. I was savouring every chorus, verse, bridge, and middle eight lyrics I wrote down. I had doubts in my mind about whether or not to show people. But my mother was so supportive. She encouraged me to show them to musicians. So that's what I did; this was when my first songwriting collaboration began.

MY FIRST SONG

I was so nervous. From what I had heard, the music industry is harsh, and I know it now; it's incredibly competitive. My first songwriting collaboration took place a long time ago. It was with songwriter, producer, and musical director Carl Simmonds, who was the musical director for Fame Factor. Carl lives not too far from me, so I arranged a meeting with him.

So many thoughts were going through my head. "Would my lyrics be good enough to put music to?" "Would a professional music industry producer work with little old, unknown me?" "Would my anxiety surrounding my speech impediment hinder working with others?" Still, my first meeting with Carl was a success; he admired my determination, and most importantly, he liked my lyrics. In the following months, Carl began to put some music to a set of my lyrics, eventually resulting in us writing a ballad, which was the first time I heard our first song. I broke down in tears. But they were tears of excitement and accomplishment.

I was starting to find myself again, growing up and

becoming more independent in following my aspirations without overthinking how my parents would continue to fight my battles for me. I was gaining enough confidence to carve my own path, taking on some battles alone and sticking up for myself. At this point in my life, I found something I could pursue for myself after football. So, the sense of belonging again started to grow inside. I happily continued honing the craft of writing lyrics, studying them, improving my form, and growing in confidence.

LEARNING TO COLLABORATE

I was introduced to songwriter and producer Jeff Rose, a brilliant guitarist who has toured with bands such as the metal band Dubwar. Again, Jeff liked my desire to keep on trying, and he loved my lyrics. This meeting resulted in us writing two rock songs together. A great experience. From there, I was introduced to another musician, songwriter, and producer, Al Steele, the guitarist in the hit-making eighties band 'The Korgis.' Over the years, we have built a strong songwriting partnership where we have written and continue to write many songs. I secretly claim to be Tim Rice. Al Steele had long searched for something with more of the music world's rock n roll humour qualities. But Tim has written lyrics to many more hits than me, so maybe I'm not quite there.

It's fair to say we are prolific as a songwriting partnership and can turn our hands to almost any music. We have written songs for Phantom of the Opera's Peter Karrie, one of our

Forces Sweethearts, Kirsten Orsborn, and many more singers. Also, it was through Al that I met the lead singer of The Korgis, James Warren, another incredible musician and songwriter who has written hit songs like 'Everybody's Got to Learn Sometime.' It is a song that never seems to go away and has been covered by the likes of Queen, Jeff Beck, and Erasure. James and I have also written a song called 'Fast and Loose,' which has now been released. It was released in Japan on a Korgis album called 'Kool Hits, Kuriosities, and Kollaborations' in August 2022 and then again in the UK that autumn.

Since way back when I started to collaborate with these incredible musicians, my connections within the music industry have grown massively, and I now collaborate with songwriters and producers worldwide, including writers from France and Portugal. As I have mentioned, the music industry is harsh, even cutthroat. Still, I am determined to follow my passion for music because it has become a massive part of my life, and I will continue to knock on every door. They say, 'If you don't ask, you don't get.' Music has made me who I am today, and I am now an author. It has changed my life. I have a desire, a sense of independence, and aspirations.

MY FIGHT FOR DISABLED MUSICIANS

I have been fortunate enough to have already connected with some incredible people within the music industry through mutual connections, making myself known on social media, and being lucky enough that my disabilities allow me to have the privilege at the moment to be able to, sometimes and when my body and mind will enable me to, get out there and network, be a visible advocate for the disability community, and introduce and show myself as being a disabled songwriter. Also, I am aware that other people's disabilities hinder them from fully participating in the everyday workings of music, such as getting to recording studios and gigs, purely because of access, and this needs to change if we are going to make music accessible for everyone.

Suppose we put our disabilities aside and stand with the other creative people trying to make it in the music industry. In that case, we need to concentrate on talent first, and it all comes down to whether or not your abilities are good enough to stand out from the millions of other songwriters, producers, and artists there are. For example, are the songs I write good enough in the present or future when pitching them to singers, TV, or film to be selected? Are the demoing vocalists singing them the right ones to be able to show prospective record labels and their artists that a particular song is good enough to invest their time and money in? These questions apply to me and any other songwriters, whether they are disabled or not.

Still, for disabled songwriters and artists to be able to become more included and more visible in the music industry, we need to create more spaces and build a barrier-free disabled songwriting and performing community where we feel safe to express ourselves and face any anxieties surrounding visibility, accessibility, and the fears about the creative and collaborative processes that come with being creative. Striking up disability songwriting and innovative partnerships foremost enable us to explore our creative limits, find out what we can achieve creatively, and then seek ways we can be able to release or publish our works. Furthermore, if we do so and feel confident enough from inside these safe spaces, introduce ways to connect with others outside the disabled community and collaborate in an integrated way, too, as I have.

This brings me to disability representation within the music industry. Whether you have a physical or learning disability, if music is in you and is part of your DNA, it will always come to the forefront. There needs to be more disability representation, not just in music but in the arts.

THE MUSICIANS UNION

With this in mind, I contacted someone from the Musicians Union, John Shortell, their Head of Equality, Diversity, and Inclusion. John is part of a committee that strives for equality and diversity in music by raising awareness through events and publications. John and his dedicated committee work tirelessly all year round to promote disabled musicians, songwriters, producers, and their members in general and to promote points raised in discussions, developing campaigns and strategies for dealing with problems like representation and access.

I asked John about these issues and asked for full permission to use them in this book.

QUESTION 1.

On the issue surrounding accessibility in the music industry as a whole and having access to wheelchair-friendly spaces such as accessible recording studios, in your opinion, what needs to happen to make the music industry more accessible for disabled songwriters and musicians?

John's Answer:
"It's a lot of work to do in education. One of the biggest barriers I hear disabled members face isn't physical, as most people would imagine, but attitudinal. Once disabled people disclose an impairment or condition, assumptions are made about what they can and can't do without any real conversation happening. This attitude limits opportunities for disabled musicians before they've even had the chance to discuss access. More exposure to disabled musicians and more visible role models would be a great way to solve that issue."

QUESTION 2.

I have cerebral palsy and a speech impediment, so my main barrier is communication and connecting personally and physically with songwriters and other people within the industry. This has been tricky. Are there any online disability songwriting communities or even accessible networking events that people may not be aware of?

. . .

John's Answer:

"Yes, The MU has a Disabled Members Network Equality Member Networks | The MU (musiciansunion.org.uk) that meet regularly and discuss issues impacting disabled musicians. The Ivor's Academy also has a working group for disabled songwriters and composers, and both Attitude is Everything and Drake Music have networks for artists to discuss issues and collaborate."

QUESTION 3.

I love songwriting, and I love to collaborate with other songwriters and musicians. But, from an educational perspective, does more need to happen? Hence, the value of disabled creatives within the industry getting a lot more representation within the music industry itself, and even from a media angle too?

John's Answer:

"The importance of vocal, visible role models must be recognised more. It's so important to see yourself or someone like you represented and hear their story. I would love to see more disabled musicians get high-profile opportunities and a platform to discuss their work. I think more needs to happen in the music education sector to make music accessible to everyone."

John Shortell, Head of Equality, Diversity & Inclusion at The Musicians Union

MY HOPES FOR DISABLED MUSICIANS

There are still evident barriers within music that must be considered to enable inclusivity, and the Musicians Union is constantly striving to advocate for ways we can collectively remove them. Seriously acting to remove the barriers, which are physical, attitudinal, and institutional, will enable disabled musicians, songwriters, and performers to become more visible and independent and will lead them to gain more freedom of choice in whichever path they choose to take in music, whether it's as a hobbyist or professional. That could be getting an education, socialising, or even simple communication. It's all about delivering the correct disability awareness, having the right mindset, vastly improving access in all areas of society, and changing stereotypes and attitudes through education. It's similar to what needs to happen in the music industry. We can achieve this by unlocking more doors and opportunities for disabled musicians and creatives, whether it's made visible from within the safe space of the disabled songwriting community or from outside it.

By making music accessible to everyone as broadly as possible and as early as possible in terms of education, we will only then start witnessing broader representation within our different communities and cultures and, most importantly, appearing more widely on our TV screens and social media. When this happens, we'll see more role models start to inspire future generations. I am happy to be that role model and advocate for both disabled and mixed-ability collaborations, which work well for me despite having disabilities. By doing this, hopefully, we can encourage more platforms to focus on what disabled creatives can bring to the music industry and music collectively and make it more diverse, as opposed to what we can't do.

SONGWRITING AND MY DISABILITIES

How we release music has changed significantly with digital technology becoming more prevalent. It's now more accessible and inclusive, and songwriters and singers can self-release music worldwide through many online platforms. In addition, streaming has revolutionised how we listen to music, making it more accessible and visible to everyone, and we need to use this to show that our music industry is accessible to everyone. I have fully realised my love for writing songs, music publishing, being creative, and working with songs.

As I discuss my disabilities in this book, I want to discuss how they affect my songwriting. Due to my physical disabilities, I haven't learned to play any instruments. I am a writer and a lyricist, and these are my strengths. This is where my collaborators step in, and they put the music to my lyrics and ideas. I love to collaborate, and collaborations within songwriting are becoming more popular, which is great, but primarily, it's all about the songwriting process that excites me.

Again, I do not mean to repeat myself, but the disability that I have that sometimes hinders or holds me back in the songwriting process the most is my speech impediment. Not being able to communicate fluently and quickly at songwriting sessions is frustrating. After all, you sometimes get asked to bare all your emotions and feelings and lay everything on the table when writing a song. Still, over the years, when writing with Al Steele in the studio, we've developed an accessible system where we work together most fluently. Before I started using augmented and alternative communication again, we would set up a laptop in the studio with a Word or Notepad document open at the ready. Then, whenever I had an idea or lyric change, I quickly typed what I was thinking onto this document so Al could promptly read it. Remember, you'll always find a way to succeed where there is a will.

So, at this point, I want to bring Al Steele into the frame, get his side of the story, and ask why he decided to collaborate with me and how he had a gut feeling that we would become such a formidable songwriting team.

AL STEELE - SHABBEY ROAD STUDIOS

Al explains in his forever happy and exuberant way,

"A few years ago, lyricist Gavin Clifton contacted me. He had already co-written with people I knew, and his stuff sounded good. So, as original music is always my preferred path, I said yes; I would love to co-write, and why didn't we try one to see how it goes?

A slight curve ball here is that Gavin has cerebral palsy and a speech impediment, which would make our communication tricky! However, being involved with The Music Man Project UK, I know the power of music over disability, and I was never one to shy away from a challenge. So Gavin and I got together to see what we could accomplish. I wanted him to have a fundamental partnership role in these songs, so to negate any communication difficulties, I set up a laptop so he could jot down if there was something I was not getting.

Gavin had several lyrics, allowing us to pick one we could efficiently work with. My studio buddy Rob Sherwood was also pitching ideas, and within an hour, we had the whole song mapped out. I then programmed the drums and put a piano down, and Rob finished the rest of the music—bass and guitars—and we then put backing vocals and a lead vocal down. The whole process took about 6 hours. We all thought we had a pretty damn good rock song, so I suggested the excellent Aubrey Parsons do the lead vocal session. A little addition of some strings, and there it was—BAM! This song is 'When Courage Shines On Me'.

Working with Gavin is always great fun, but he is undoubtedly not a silent partner. He always comes with influences and ideas for where we can take a song. Sometimes, we are writing to a brief, which means we have to adapt what we have to make the song fit. Sometimes, a new artist will record an existing song, and it is great that we can adjust a lyric or a feel to suit that artist.

Gavin is an inspiration to all who work with him. He never complains, and if someone says, 'You can't do that,' Gavin will say, 'Oh yes, I can!' Long may we continue to write together, and long may Gavin continue to be a role model to others, those with a disability and those without."

Al Steele - Shabbey Road Studios/The Korgis

YOU ONLY LEARN BY DOING

My knowledge of the songwriting side of the industry has gone from strength to strength. I always say, 'you only learn by doing,' and by jumping into a recording studio writing environment, I have learned the fundamental ins and outs of music and songwriting and met many other songwriters. Despite this, I know that, having a disability, like when I was in employment, I will always have that imposter syndrome feeling lingering over me. Still, the truth is, there is always someone better than you at something in everything we choose to turn our hands and minds to; they can do things better and, off the back of this, have spent time perfecting their skillset through talent, hard work, and lots of studies. Whether you have a disability or not, the truth is, there will always be someone better than you; that's life.

It's the same in the music industry. There are artists, songwriters, and producers who have honed their craft and are better than you, meaning that they are at the top of their game and leading the way with writing, producing, and releasing songs. Still, this doesn't mean that opportunities aren't there for disabled songwriters. I have been fortunate enough to go to recording studios, collaborate with hit songwriters, and have songs placed with artists. I want to use my continuing songwriting journey to encourage and inspire others who are disheartened or discouraged when pursuing a disability songwriting path to never give up because that one door to success may open. You are not alone, and as a music community, now is the time to start building up the correct communities we all feel safe in, become willing to integrate them where it's in our best interests, support each other, and make music more inclusive for everyone within it.

CHAPTER 7
THE AUTHOR

"Disability is natural. We must stop believing that disabilities keep a person from doing something. Because that's not true... Having a disability doesn't stop me from doing anything." — **Benjamin Snow**

HOW MAX AND THE MAGIC WISH CAME ABOUT

For most of my life, I had always dreamed of being a children's book author; for a long time, my parents always told me to write a children's book. But other things seemed to overshadow this dream for many years. As a result, I was juggling the many things I was doing before sitting down and writing my first one, Max and the Magic Wish.

I was growing up, having operations, dealing with

epilepsy, learning to walk, coping with my speech impediment, and striving to get my voice heard while navigating through my school years. Then, I decided where I wanted to go with my education before eventually working at a newspaper for seventeen years and finally finding it within my soul to begin trying to start one day. Still, it wasn't until sometime after I had written Max and the Wish that I realised I needed to get to a place where at least I could start understanding the link between self-acceptance and being ready to get to a position where I could start loving my disabilities after lengthy conversations with my children's book collaborator, illustrator, and publisher, Clare Thomas. Yes, I had written this children's book, but truthfully, I needed clarification on the real reason why. I was like a lost child, and honestly, I sometimes think of that famous Peter Pan quote, 'Forget them, Wendy. Forget them all. Come with me, where you'll never have to worry about grown-up things again.' When I think about how my life has turned out, I'm still a big kid at heart, just one who overthinks. I should think less like Peter Pan.

I had written my true story about a particular part of my life but didn't know how I would use it to make a difference. All I knew was that I had written a children's book. It was like flying a plane without getting my pilot's licence. I had no sense of direction or meaning. I want to take you back to when Max and the Magic Wish was just a manuscript. I had initially pitched my manuscript to book publishers and literary agents for many months. During these months, I received rejection after rejection. I was at a loss for what to do.

I attended a music industry showcase evening where Clare, a singer/songwriter who's worked for record labels and sung all over the world, was a talent mentor. But, again, we didn't speak at the music industry event due to my anxieties about my speech impediment. A few weeks later, I remember reaching out to her on social media purely from a songwriting perspective. As we continued to message each other, Clare said she writes, illustrates, and publishes children's books, and then I explained how it was my dream to have my story published, and this was when I sent my manuscript over to Clare.

It wasn't until a week later that Clare messaged me, asking if we could meet and discuss my story. We met outside a local pub, and my mother came with me for support in case Clare couldn't understand my speech. We chatted for a while, getting to know each other and telling each other about our creative pasts. It was then, a few days after this, that Clare messaged me, giving me the news I honestly wasn't expecting due to getting rejected by so many book publishers. Yes, this was the moment I became a published author. My dreams were finally coming true.

Boy, didn't I know this was just the start? I still needed to understand the amount of work involved with becoming an author. But truthfully, this has been the best thing to happen to me for a long time. Meeting Clare has made me a better and different person. She is one of the most humble people I have met, and I am so glad she walked into my life back then. But, of course, people come and go in your lifetime, and you learn something new from each person on their journey. But, these past few years, I have grown up (well, a little) and found my purpose in life. I've found my dream, added to it, and turned it up a notch, and I'm living it and will continue to do so.

LEARNING THE AUTHOR'S ROPES

Becoming an author takes time, and there's a lot you need to embrace if you want longevity. It's like learning how to ride your first bicycle. You learn day by day, peddle by peddle. You fell; get back up. You make mistakes and learn from them, which I have done until now. Nobody is perfect; you'll never become the complete author, and you will come to embrace this over time.

In one of our early meetings, Clare asked me what my aspirations were for my first book. I replied, To become a bestselling children's book author. I now know how partly correct I was in my answer because, although I am now a bestselling children's book author, it's not something I achieved alone. It takes a lot of hard work to accomplish a bestselling book. Please don't think I wrote a story, published it, and made it a bestseller. It doesn't work like that.

How wrong was I for not figuring out why I wanted to write this book? At this point, I still wasn't being true to myself. Even though I had written about disability and acceptance, I hadn't accepted that the message in the book was one that, deep down in my soul, I was consciously fighting and hiding, even though I was still a kid in the story. It was as if who I was hadn't been clarified in my mind. Clare could sense this and knew she had to make me realise this before we moved on to editing, developmental editing, illustrating, and publishing. It was the lasting wake-up call I desperately needed, along with the trigger for me to finally step onto an open road journey to accepting myself as a disabled adult and falling in love with who I am.

In the following weeks, Clare and I locked ourselves away. Within that time, I learned a lot about myself, children's books, writing techniques, story structures, character building, emotions, and becoming an author. It was all so overwhelming, but I'm happy about those times. Clare pushed me to my limits, and I am now much more knowledgeable about being an author. It's full-on, full-time, and you must be patient and passionate about everything associated with authorship.

After copious drafts, re-drafts, edits, developmental editing, and designing, the writing stages of Max and the Magic Wish were complete. The next step was for Clare to move on to the illustration. I knew what style of illustration I wanted. You've guessed it: big, bright, colourful, and bold. I love illustrations that complement my personality: loud, bright, colourful, and funny. My inspiration for this comes from another children's book author, David Walliams. Clare, being the talented soul she is, went away and locked herself away for days, weeks, and the following months. Drawing each watercolour character from nothing, the inspiration for my character came from a childhood photo I had sent to her. For the rest of the characters, Clare drew from nothing. She is an exceptional talent; honestly, the first time I saw what she had come up with, I cried tears of joy. Our characters are beautiful. Seeing myself become a character was like looking into a mirror of my past. Clare has captured and squeezed my personality into Max so elegantly. My actual pet dog, Max, served as inspiration for Max.

THE RELEASE OF MY FIRST CHILDREN'S BOOK

My dream of becoming a published author was getting closer, and reality was looming. With the story written, the draft and editing stages are complete. The only tasks left were for Clare to design the front and back covers, design the book's layout, and send complimentary copies out to beta readers to get feedback on our masterpiece before we published. So, the publication date was set for October 29, 2020. The excitement was building, and the nerves were on edge.

Releasing a children's book is so different from releasing a song. A song has peaks and troughs; although songs never get old, those peaks happen quickly. With a book, it's all about longevity, and it took me a while to get my head around this because, up until this point, I had only worked with releasing songs. When the 29th of October 2020 arrived, I was nervous. All I had in my head was that I would get enough sales and momentum behind me to get into the Amazon Top Twenty. I can honestly say now that I was being so egotistical and how wrong it was for me to think this way, and that my attitude has completely changed. I now know that the most important thing for me as an author is that it's all about making a difference for children and parents with disabilities. Deep down, I believed this, but I wasn't prepared to admit it, and I am so grateful to Clare for breaking me down and showing me this because my stubbornness engulfed me again. It had me, and I didn't want to show it.

In the following months, book sales steadily increased. We were selling. When you are an author, the process never stops. By this, I mean that writing your story and getting it published is the aim, but so much more needs to be done after you've published it, and you continuously need to have your foot firming on the gas. The press release and media kit must be put together and distributed; website design and upkeep; book signings, interviews, and podcasts; arranging to get your stock in; and most importantly, promotion and promotion. It's only possible to publish a book if you let people know you've written one.

WORKING WITH BBC BROADCASTER LUCY OWEN

Around November 2021, a friend, Michael Donovan, contacted me, saying that a charity he knew wanted to do an author spotlight on me. As part of this, he had arranged for the Welsh news broadcaster Lucy Owen to read my book virtually to hundreds of schoolchildren in the Merthyr Tydfil area. This day was extraordinary for me, seeing so many children interact with Max and The Magic Wish. It was one of my most memorable days as an author so far. After the event, Michael passed my email address on to Lucy Owen. She shortly after contacted me, asking if I was happy to be interviewed on television for BBC Wales Today. Naturally, as I accepted, my anxiety went through the roof. I explained to her how I used a communication aid and could pre-record any answers to any questions she wanted to ask me as voiceovers. Then, I asked her to send me her interview questions sometime before we filmed the interview at The Bank Coffee Shop in South Wales with my father, Martin, and publisher Clare Thomas.

Being interviewed was one of my life's scariest yet most enjoyable experiences. It was emotional, with my father ending up in tears whilst being interviewed, and I know Clare was an emotional wreck, too. Still, the interview aired on BBC Wales Today on the International Day of Disabilities. We highlighted how I wanted to make a difference by writing my story. Shortly after, Max and the Magic Wish became an Amazon bestseller. Now, after having experience appearing on television, I would not change anything because I know that falling in love with your disabilities is paramount to staying true to who you are. By doing this, you will begin to inspire others about the importance of broadly representing all kinds of disabilities within society. The key to this becoming the norm is education through the media, schools, and especially children's books.

LEARNING HOW TO PROMOTE MYSELF AS AN AUTHOR

Social media and a website are critical elements to getting yourself out there as an author. Posting frequently on Facebook, Instagram, and TikTok helps drive sales and traffic to the likes of Amazon and your website. SEO and keywords are relevant to your niche, which in my case is being a writer, disability advocate, and blogger. Use the correct keywords within your website, and in these modern times, TikTok gets you noticed and drives traffic towards your website, translating into book sales. I've learned this the hard way, and I am still learning. Admittedly, my confidence in my speech is far from where I would like it to be. Still, I have now started to get out there more. I am now beginning to attend networking events. Do more book signings and meet-and-greet events. But, outside of this, your online presence will be your focal point, especially with how the world is going, which is technology-driven.

Jumping back to when we were amid the COVID pandemic Clare and I were still meeting virtually, and during this time, we discussed how I could show my diversity as a writer and an author. As well as writing children's books about disability and acceptance, I've always wanted to write some short magical and adventure stories. So, being locked down during the pandemic for such long periods, I set about doing that and writing a magical adventure story. But I didn't stop there and write one story. I've now written eight short magical and adventure stories, one of which was Paddy the Polar Bear Teddy, published in December 2021. Again, Clare and I worked together on developmental editing, character development, and story structure. Once again, Clare illustrated and designed the book. My second children's book was published on November 30, 2021. Paddy, the Polar Bear Teddy, differs entirely from Max and The Magic Wish. Clare's illustrations complement the educational message of Max and The Magic Wish, which is about disability and acceptance. Paddy, the Polar Bear Teddy, is a magical adventure story for older children. I let their imaginations run wild while taking them through many of the emotional lessons we learn while growing up, like friendship, being courageous when needed, and using wisdom to be kind to others.

ADVICE FOR BUDDING AUTHORS

I want to give any new author advice. That's to have a clear idea of what to write. Make sure you are passionate about it, follow your heart, and pitch your story and ideas to other authors, publishers, and literary agents because they are the people you'll learn from. Not everyone might be as lucky as me to have someone like Clare, who helped guide me through this process. Develop, edit, illustrate, and format my book and publish my story. However, you never know where your writing endeavours may lead you. Remember, it's about sustaining longevity as an author and a passion. It's about making a difference and leaving people with a lasting lesson or message about something you care about. It's about always being true to yourself and your values and using these to educate all generations using life's experiences and learning from those experiences. Remember that.

We also need to talk more openly about diversity in book publishing, which is becoming more widely discussed. Still, the focus regularly seems to be on other diverse and marginalised sectors like mental health and racism, the LGBTQ community, and human rights. The disabled community is the largest minority group in the world. However, when you search for books representative of disability in general or written about a targeted disability or audience, your search can go on forever and usually ends up with you finding no books on the subject you are looking for. The same applies to disabled children's books. There are very few out there, and naturally, when we are young, we are most inquisitive. Children always ask questions, and how they learn by reading books represents who they are. This is when problematic subjects like disability can become part of the educational conversation you have as a family.

I believe the focus must also be shifted towards disabled people writing disabled books and creating characters based on real-life issues. Scenarios that disabled persons experience daily, just like my storyline in Max and The Magic Wish. Its storyline is based on a situation I had to grow up dealing with, becoming accepted for who I am, and showing others how to deal with all the emotional barriers and characteristics within the story. Of course, nothing is stopping non-disabled authors from creating disabled characters. Still, there's a strong argument that they may get disconnected and misinterpret the real challenges and emotions that disabled people endure.

There are already some other incredibly talented disabled authors around. We are a minority but a force to be reckoned with because we are playing our part in leading the way regarding disability education and awareness. Still, I firmly believe that the book publishing industry still needs to unite and become more allies with disabled authors, just like my incredible publisher, Clare, who fully supports me in everything I do author-wise. It takes a lot to bare all and write about our sensitive disability problems and how the unforgiving, inaccessible world around us puts up many barriers that hinder us from living the best lives we can. Disabled people share their sensitive and emotional experiences to educate others and make a difference. But to help us sustain longevity as authors, we need to be supported in our creative endeavours and given an equal platform to get our work out there to keep doing what we love financially, which is to write.

CLARE THOMAS - BOOK PUBLISHER/ILLUSTRATOR

It's always challenging to be the publisher and the friend. Sometimes, you are afraid of overstepping the mark when discussing the next steps for the book or projects because there's always a fine line. Knowing how honest to be with someone is extremely hard and even more complicated when someone like Gavin has such high expectations. You don't want him to believe he can't do it because of his disability, but eventually, I have to become the big, bad publisher rather than the friend to get things done.

There's no surprise when I tell you that Gavin can be very stubborn and determined. I'm sure you've grasped that from reading this book already. However, my journey with Gavin has most definitely been an interesting one. I want to say life-changing.

Our First Meeting

I wasn't concerned about his speech impediment when I first met Gavin. I grasped what he was saying or trying to say early on. If I needed help understanding, I would ask him to write it down. I treated our meeting just like any other meeting I'd previously had. However, most of my meetings don't start on a pub bench. Somewhere, Gavin feels right at home.

When I received Gavin's story, Max and the Magic Wish, I loved it. I could see the potential it had to make a difference. Help children understand disability from all perspectives. I had just finished working with another Welsh children's author, illustrating his new book, so I was ready to jump into another project. Max seemed perfect—an important project I wanted to help publish.

I set up another meeting for Gavin to come by my office to discuss the next steps and his hopes and dreams for the book. I wanted to learn about and understand who Gavin was and why he was doing what he was doing. I can still remember Gavin's first words as he entered the room.

"I want a number-one bestselling book." He said. All before he had even sat down. I remember laughing aloud and thinking he had no idea what that would take.

We had a few more meetings at my office; I called them developmental editing meetings, where we sat down and took the story of Max apart. It was so important to get a story like Max's right. Gavin had a chance to make a difference and help change views on disability, so we worked for months to perfect his story and illustration ideas until they were right. But after several meetings, I couldn't shake the feeling that Gavin didn't identify as having a disability. Now, you are probably thinking, What is she talking about? He has a visible disability. I often told myself I was being silly, but I knew Gavin didn't see himself as having cerebral palsy.

I asked him if he saw himself as disabled, and he replied, 'No.' His answer left me shocked, confused, and, more importantly, worried about how Gavin would promote a book on disability if he didn't see his disability. Gavin explained how he sees himself as 'one of the boys' and doesn't like to think of himself as having cerebral palsy. I will be honest; at this point, I was ready to give up on Max because I've always believed an author brand is essential to why books sell. Readers fall in love with the author because of their authenticity and struggles. How would we sell a book on disability if the author didn't see himself as disabled?

I won't lie. I struggled with it, maybe because I didn't

understand it. How could Gavin write such a beautiful story and want to make a difference for those with cerebral palsy but not identify as having the same disability? We sat for hours talking about it. Gavin explained how he hates being seen as disabled. I knew he would joke about it, but I could see the anxiety it gave him. I remember trying to reassure him that there was nothing wrong with him. He should be proud of who he is and what he tries to do.

These conversations left me questioning 'why' Gavin wished to publish his book. If I was going to illustrate, edit, format, and publish a big project like Max, I wanted to be sure that Gavin was working on his mindset to be ready to promote and market a great story. So we set about building Gavin's author brand. Finding out his author's vision, voice, audience, how he wants his readers to perceive him, what his mission was, his values, and everything else that could help Gavin become the best version of himself and, hopefully, fall in love with himself I like to call it author therapy.

Watching Gavin grow was magical

Those months of hard work on his part most definitely helped. Witnessing someone grow and fall in love with themselves right before you is pretty special. I'll be the first to admit I had to be tough on Gavin, but that was because I knew releasing a book on a subject such as cerebral palsy, teamed with Gavin's expectations and goals, wouldn't go down well with Gavin if it didn't make an impact. If we hadn't worked hard for Gavin to understand the world he was venturing into, it would have been like throwing him into a pack of wolves. I didn't want that for him. The whole reason for publishing Max was to make a difference. That would only happen if Gavin were the best version of himself and ready for whatever was coming.

Well, it came in droves—newspapers, TV, blogs, charities, and a number-one Amazon bestseller book label. Yes, what Gavin asked for in our first meeting in my office finally happened through sheer determination and hard work. We both achieved what we set out to do: Gavin as the author, and I as the illustrator and publisher. I was proud of the great team we had become. But more proud that during this whole process, Gavin had fallen in love with his disability instead of feeling ashamed of it.

Lesson Learnt

Unfortunately, Gavin still had a lot of work to do for himself. One incident after the book launch was Gavin's offer to appear on an American podcast promoting his book. I reminded him that he would have to talk to the host, which would be difficult for him to do. I advised him to only podcast if there were pre-recorded questions from the host to allow him to participate in the conversation. The podcast was a disaster. We logged on—Gavin from his home and me from my office. The host said hello, and as soon as Gavin replied, the host looked confused. Yes, Gavin had not told the host he had a speech impediment.

At that moment, I felt a little mad. The host needed help figuring out what to do on the spot, as it was being recorded live. It was a good thing that I knew Gavin and the book well, because I ended up doing all the talking for an hour. Still, the point I made to Gavin was that you have to be honest with people—especially those who run podcasts or radio. I sensed he was disappointed that night. I believe he thought the host had treated him unfairly. But I disagreed. Gavin wanted to feel normal and partake in a podcast so badly that he couldn't admit his disability. He didn't need to be ashamed that he had a speech impediment; he just needed to find alternative ways that worked for him while being honest. I know Gavin learned a lot from that night. He's actually featured on another podcast with pre-recorded questions, and it was fantastic. He now doesn't go anywhere without his laptop. A lesson well learned.

After the success of Max and the Magic Wish came Paddy the Polar Bear Teddy. Another collaborative book we had so much fun working on. Unfortunately, Paddy was released right in the heart of COVID-19, so any promotional events couldn't take place. It was a challenging time. However, it was a time when Gavin discovered social media, and it became his best friend. Gavin got to work building his true fanbase. I was incredibly proud to see how he put himself out there, embracing his disability instead of denying it. Once again, watching him grow and flourish on camera was a true privilege.

All Good things come to an end

As I sit here writing my part for Gavin's book, I reflect on our journey thus far. I'm proud to have worked on all three books with Gavin. After a year of planning and developmental editing, Gavin would send each chapter over, and I'd send them back with revisions. Sending Gavin back to the drawing board over and over because he imagined he grew up in the 50s working down the Welsh pits—honestly, I'm not kidding. In the first chapter of this book, Gavin was Tom Jones. We laughed a lot during the process. It was a lot of fun. He worked incredibly hard to bring you what you are reading. However, I have decided to pass the reigns over to Gavin to self-publish this book himself. Although I have loved every minute of working with Gavin, it is time for him to fly and work on bigger and better things. I wish him all the best with the book and his future.

Clare Thomas - Lola & Co Publishing

HOW MAX AND THE MAGIC WISH BECAME AN AUDIOBOOK

In today's book market, the need to release the same book in different formats puts you at the cutting edge of the market, and releasing your work in other forms is the most appealing. We released 'Max and the Magic Wish' as a paperback, quickly followed by the eBook. Still, looking into the future and the world becoming very tech-driven, Clare and I were keen to investigate ways to enter the audiobook market. I am passionate about this book reaching and educating many children, whatever their abilities are. Suppose this meant that by releasing an audiobook version, children with disabilities like visual impairments and learning disabilities could be included in the experience of reading 'Max and the Magic Wish'. By listening to the audiobook, the concept, desire, and reason why I wrote this story are becoming a dream come true. It warms my heart that I can make a difference in these children's lives.

After buying a copy of 'Max and the Magic Wish' and reading my story, I received a lovely message on Facebook from a friend named Kate. Kate couldn't stress enough how much my book had touched her. She asked if I would let her narrate the book as an audiobook. I first met Kate at a local charity gig she had organised, a spectacular West End Musical Theatre-themed concert, where I watched Kate showcase one of her other talents, singing. I already knew how talented she was, so I did not doubt that she would do fantastic narration and hone in on the different characteristics of each character every step of the way in the story. Kate is a genuine diamond. She most definitely shines bright. She would not only be an asset to any musical or theatre production but also as a singer, recording artist, and most certainly a voiceover artist or narrator. Thank you so much for working with us, Kate.

Kate says,

"Thank you so, so much, Gavin. It's been a pleasure and a privilege to record your beautiful book. Thank you for allowing me to be involved. :-) xxx"

GAVIN, THE DISABLED BLOGGER

Consider other writing avenues when thinking of becoming an author. It's probably in your interest to take these other avenues of creative writing seriously because you build your following of loyal supporters by looking at different writing methods. It works, too. When Clare, my publisher, introduced me to disability blogging, I didn't understand why she pushed me in that direction. Still, I wouldn't do without it nowadays because it's a great way of attracting leads and followers in a way that doesn't cost you lots of money. All you need to start blogging and attracting followers this way is a website, which costs a monthly subscription fee but is well worth the small investment in the long run.

For a few years, I was reluctant to blog. The thought of laying my soul on the line and telling the world about my life with cerebral palsy was daunting. But now, I write about it without even thinking about any negative or ableist backlash because I now know that, with my age and my experience of having to live in a world not built in so many ways for many disabled people, In terms of representation and access, which I've excessively spoken about throughout this book, I can inspire and educate many people.

Admittedly, until I found it in my soul to fall in love with my disabilities, I was not too fond of the thought of inspiring others. I was thinking, in one sense, why should disabled people be seen as inspirational? Please don't assume that it's our fault that we were born different. Still, the journey I've come through the past few years has made me realise that there is massive scope everywhere for generational and societal attitudes to change forever because, moving forward, the internet and social media can become so educational.

I was constantly afraid of online trolls and being their target before I started blogging. Still, since I bit the bullet and started my blog, I have learned that these trolls and so-called keyboard warriors do what they do out of jealousy and fear of living in more diverse times. My father clarified this notion by reminding me of how many young children with many disabilities I am inspiring and showing that you can live a successful life even if you have differences and disabilities. Therefore, whenever I am having a bad day or feel down, I remember that in our lives, we all make a difference to someone every day, and bad people are not the ones we need in our lives, but people who do good are precious to us. Without a doubt, we need more disabled people to tell their stories, whether through television and the media, social media, or blogging.

I want to encourage disabled people to give blogging a try because when we tell our stories of disability, that's when we educate others. Educating others can make a difference in a broader society, and when we start making a difference, we help our world become more inclusive. By becoming a disability blogger, I got the exciting opportunity to write disability articles for the Metro Opinion platform. They allow people from diverse backgrounds to write about their life experiences and air their opinions, creating a space for discussing many complex topics.

WRITING FOR METRO OPINION

On a cold winter evening, wrapped up in my duvet, scrolling through social media, I stumbled across a post from a well-known disability celebrity, author, and advocate saying that The Metro was looking for more disabled writers and columnists. So again, this would be another excellent writing outlet and a great way to show people another side of my creative writing and a more serious side. So, I immediately emailed the designated contact, Jess Austin, the First-Person and Opinion Editor for the Metro, introducing myself and including some of the blogs I had already published on my blog. Within a couple of days, Jess replied, telling me that she liked what I had written and was advocating for, and asked if I was happy for her to edit my blogs ready for publication on the Metro

Opinion website. Writing articles for a national publication has been so good for my confidence. Admittedly, there have been a few offensive comments on my articles from keyboard warriors. Still, again, I choose to ignore them, strengthening me, affirming how far I have come, continuing the process of falling in love with my disabilities, and mentally learning to become more resilient.

I want to say a massive thank you to The Metro Opinion and Jess for working with me this far and for publishing my heartfelt opinions on disability. You have given me a national outlet where I can continue to air my views and stories about living with cerebral palsy and where I can endeavour to make a difference to others. For legal and clarity reasons, I want to disclaim that I have used and referenced content from some of my published Metro.co.uk articles in this book.

BECOMING AN AUTHOR WAS ALWAYS MY DESTINY

If you rewind my life and look back, I was always destined to become a writer, and fulfilling my dream of becoming an author has verified this. But, as for Clare and me coming together, was this some incident waiting to happen? Did fate play its hand over many years? They say that those difficult discussions you have in life, especially ones taken out of your hands in my case, lead you to new and more extraordinary things. Becoming a full-time writer and author has changed my life. It has made me a better person, changed my life, and given me a purpose. It has also helped me step onto a journey to get to a place where I may fall in love with my disabilities and find the 'real Gavin.' The one who has always been someone who needed to just search deep down inside to just accept that I am a disabled, funny, caring person.

I am now making a difference through the power of writing, and from a personal perspective, I would advise others with disabilities that if they like to write, to go for it, let their creative flair excel, and use it as a helpful tool. It will guide and help you in many ways. It can be a powerful way of expressing yourself, even if you feel you cannot physically speak out about how your disabilities affect you. It can help improve cognitive function, fine motor skills, and hand-eye coordination. It gives you a platform, a voice, and an outlet and can allow you to express your genuine inner emotions in a powerful, safe, and creative way.

CHAPTER 8
THE SCEPTIC

"I'm an over-thinker, and being different can cause you some depression." —Gavin Clifton

My biggest downfall in any part of my journey so far has been self-doubt and the fear of the unknown. I may seem confident when I am around others, and most of the time, I am. Still, being different and knowing that I sometimes need help communicating, doing the odd everyday chore, or travelling alone scares me. I love getting out into the heart of society and showing that being accepted for who you are is perfectly ok. I love networking, attending events, and signing books, but I occasionally find these occasions difficult and even tiring when doing them on my own.

My parents accompany me to these events whenever they can. My mother attends most of my book signing events, and my father attends most of my music events. But it's tough because I know my parents are getting older and won't be around forever. They have their own lives to live, and I want them to enjoy their, let's say, 'limelight' (lol) years of retirement as much as they can.

I get frustrated when I can't represent myself or attend events alone. I could look at getting a part-time personal assistant to accompany me at these events, but hiring personal assistants costs money, which in this day and age isn't financially sensible.

The other issue that worries me is that some people may exploit disabled people. May that be physical or financial. I often worry about travelling the country alone and driving hundreds of miles. Would I cope staying in hotels alone, and are there even enough accessible hotel rooms everywhere to stay in hotels safely? Like I said before, being disabled, you often overthink and play out scenarios in your mind, and now, thinking about it, I have been too dignified in the past because of this, and like so many other men, I have been too proud and stubborn to speak out about my mental health.

MY ASPIRATIONS

Despite having some regrets, not by my own doing but because of the barriers within our society that prevent me from travelling and possibly living my aspirations, this is when my parents remind me of all of my achievements thus far. How I am inspiring and showing others with disabilities that, despite having many ableist barriers around us, you can succeed with determination, resources, and patience Since we have come out of the pandemic, my perseverance and desire to get out there and represent myself and the disability community have grown massively. I am now at an age where I need to grow a pair. I now know that I am and can make a difference by educating others by just being my bonkers self and getting out there.

Thinking back to when I was a teenager, I didn't have a care in the world. But I do not doubt that as you get older, you become more aware of how you are seen, and sometimes fear takes over and you worry about things more. You worry about how you are perceived and sometimes try too hard to fit into society, then fall into the trap of trying to please everyone, even more so because you know you are seen as different. However, being locked down during the pandemic for so long helped me. It allowed me to discover who I was years ago and who I want to be now. My anxiety was getting the better of me, and I now know the fear of getting trolled in the community, primarily online, was taking hold of me because I wanted to follow my dreams and become an author. How stupid I was for letting this get to me.

I'M NOT AFRAID TO GET OUT THERE

I have now rediscovered Gavin and am enjoying life more than ever. I'm now not afraid to speak up for what I believe in, and I'm certainly not scared of blocking any idiotic keyboard warriors on social media.

I am now becoming more confident in my skin. I am working towards falling in love with myself again, and I'm currently in a place where I'm not so afraid to be seen and get out there, so much so that I've even thrown myself into networking.

Networking is where brands and businesses meet and discuss or pass on opportunities. It's a fantastic way of helping others and growing your brand. I have had opportunities open up for me. If I hadn't found the confidence to get out there this way, I wouldn't have encountered these opportunities and, most importantly, met many wonderful people.

Finding my youthful (I wish) confidence and leaving my sceptical woes in the past, I'm now not afraid to get out there and be visual once again. By doing this, I can make a difference in some capacity. However, I'm not under the illusion that I can change the world and its attitude towards making society more equal and accessible. I'm not Superman, after all. Still, if I can inspire the people willing to listen and become more educated on how we can all become included, this journey I'm riding and even writing this book are justified.

NETWORKING

Since networking, I have been connected and introduced to many wonderful people, like news broadcaster Lucy Owen from BBC Wales Today. Lucy interviewed me for a special broadcast on December 3, 2021. December 3rd is the annual celebration of the International Day of Persons With Disabilities. It promotes the rights of people with disabilities in all areas of society. The interview consisted of my father, Martin, and my publisher, Clare, being interviewed by Lucy Owen. We talked about my life growing up with cerebral palsy, my true story of disability and acceptance, the story behind 'Max and the Magic Wish,' and my journey so far as an author.

Networking has brought people back into my life. They say life works and moves in mysterious ways. One day, I was at a networking event in Newport and bumped into two people I hadn't talked to in such a long time. It's been fantastic reconnecting with them after all these years. Since that day, we have continued to stay in touch and attend networking events together. Their support has been exceptional, and I cannot thank them enough.

VISITING THE SENEDD

Clare and I were fortunate to accompany them to The Senedd in Cardiff Bay to promote my first children's book, Max and the Magic Wish, and its message about disability and acceptance. The Senedd is a government office here in Wales where the devolved Welsh government debates Welsh policies and makes laws for Wales. During our visit, we met with Laura Ann Jones, a Member of the Senedd and a Conservative politician serving South East Wales, to discuss possibly getting my children's book into Welsh schools to help make a difference in the lives of children not only with cerebral palsy but all kinds of disabilities. We visited the member's tea room, where Laura Ann Jones, MS, and her assistant were waiting to meet us. They were lovely and accommodating, and our meeting lasted around half an hour.

First, Laura welcomed each one of us before we sat around a table to discuss ways on how we can get my children's book Max and the Magic Wish out to schools in Wales to help make a difference in the lives of children not only with cerebral palsy but all kinds of disabilities. I believe having resources like Max and the Magic Wish in our Welsh schools will add to the amount of disability awareness we need to get out there to change lives and also the mindsets of everyone by educating people that it's perfectly ok to be different.

I even got to play a pre-recorded speech to Laura, which I had previously recorded using my AAC communication aid. She was so patient and engaged. She listened to my every word. I am glad to report that the entire meeting went well and was constructive.

Laura Ann Jones, MP, explained,

"It was fantastic to meet with Gavin, who has an incredible

passion for inspiring children with disabilities and their parents. Max and the Magic Wish is a triumph, not just for Gavin but for disabled people across the UK. I look forward to supporting his campaign to make the book an essential resource for all children and parents."

Our visit to the Senedd was by no means an ordinary day. Let's start by rewinding to the evening before, when we all received an email from one of Laura's staff letting us know that there would be a high-profile VIP present at The Senedd at the same time as our visit. Yes, someone even more important than us, lol. So, we were all asked to provide identification to ensure we were who we said we were. Luckily, we were all deemed legit.

As we arrived in Cardiff, we noticed a much higher level of security than would typically be present. We drove to the location where security asked us to park in an accessible parking area, where the car was stringently checked over by security before we were escorted to our parking space and then into a lift. Curious. We asked who the high-profile VIP visitor was, and at this moment we were informed that Prince William, the Prince of Wales, was present in the building. As we entered The Senedd via the Ty Hywel offices because the main entrance was closed, we endured further tight security checks by being asked to walk through airport-style walk-through metal detectors. It wasn't for lack of trying, but unfortunately, we didn't get to meet him in person, but to be in the same building as a royal was an exciting feeling nonetheless.

I'M LEARNING TO ACCEPT MY DIFFERENCES

Overthinking too often and worrying about looking different and being treated differently can make you feel depressed and alone. Stupidly, in the past, there have been times when I dealt with the issues I have talked about in this chapter by trapping and keeping them deep inside me. But, where there was no need to, I've now learned that talking about your differences openly and learning to accept them, even though it's one of the most challenging things I had to do, is the best thing you can do. I was worried that nobody would understand how vital it is to come to terms with these differences. Still, there's no hiding from your differences, and I want to reassure anybody going through this that you are not alone.

The process of accepting yourself will take however long it needs to. So, please don't do it alone. Speak to someone. It takes time to fall in love with your disabilities. So take all the time you need to find the strength to love your body. Living with cerebral palsy has been challenging. Still, I've worked so hard on letting the rigid walls that I have tended to surround myself with for many years, even though I didn't let them show very often, fall from around me—almost all of them anyway.

Accepting yourself as disabled can take time. However, whenever you accept yourself for who you are, you will find it within yourself to let the good things and fun times in your life become even more important. Whenever you experience difficult times, the good stuff and fun memories you make will make you a stronger person than ever and drive you on with a more purposeful mindset. Look at how far I have come. I am now writing my autobiography, I go to networking events by myself, I'm comfortable in front of a camera, I have written two children's books, and I'm not afraid to upset anyone by standing up for disability rights. I'm not scared of getting trolled because I now block any keyboard warriors. I now realise that I need allies, not enemies, to continue to make a difference in the world.

Since becoming an author and realising why I always wanted to write Max and the Magic Wish, I can make a difference. Showing others wholeheartedly that discovering the inner belief that has likely always been inside can be the catalyst for accepting yourself and letting yourself accept others As a result, I have become more confident from within, and I have accepted myself as a disabled person more and more. Still, I have my bad moments of anxiety, and that's ok. We are allowed a bit of downtime and are only humans. However, doing this has allowed me to find a new level of self-confidence and become more determined to never give up on what I love: writing and enjoying life as often as possible with my family and friends.

MIRROR ACTIVITY

Another simple everyday activity I have yet to be too keen on is looking in the mirror, especially at the lower half of my body and seeing my wonky legs. It seems like you are in a dream, transported to another world where you are at the circus, and everywhere you turn, you see those funhouse mirrors that distort your reflected image. I am pretty funny, but I don't think I could get a job as a circus clown. I'd have a reflection and reaction complex. I couldn't keep still, even though I was jumpy when not looking at myself in the mirror. Hence, I never watch horror movies. I'd be stuck to the ceiling by the time the movie ended.

I am happier now seeing myself in a mirror, though, and I am confident enough to go on camera, whether for a disability news film, documentary, or social media. You can't keep me away from the camera these days.

Here's how I deal with looking in the mirror, which works: I use a simple mind trick. When you see yourself staring back in the opposite mirror, try not to focus too much on the parts you primarily dislike about your body.

For example, I hated looking at my legs in the mirror. Therefore, I concentrate on aspects of my body that my parents or people who know me best say are attractive, like my blue eyes. I looked straight down at my legs for a long while, becoming even more anxious about their appearance. But by looking myself straight in the eyes consciously right away, I instantly remembered what my parents said, meaning that positive thoughts were the first thing that entered my head. These positive thoughts seem to continue as I eventually look at other parts of my body. Every time I look at my legs in the mirror now, I try to remember that they are just another beautiful part of who I am, even though they differ from most people's legs.

FACING FEARS

Also, remember that with every video, film, documentary, or social media post about your disabilities, You are always making a difference, inspiring others, and showing others that being disabled doesn't mean you cannot live to the best of your abilities. Ok, you may need to do certain things and chores differently from others, but that's ok. So, let me tell you another secret: one of my worst fears was getting trolled and receiving hateful comments on social media for a long time. But I know now that there is no need to be scared of any trolls and to not let them stop you from inspiring and educating other people about different kinds of disabilities.

By telling your story, you are helping society become more educated, open, and inclusive, especially when discussing disabilities. After all, what's there to be scared about? There's always a report and block button on these social media platforms to handle unwanted trolling.

So, if you are at a point where you dislike looking at yourself in the mirror or being on camera because of your disabilities and how you look, it's perfectly normal not to ever be totally in love with what you see. Nobody is perfect, and I fully understand the fear of seeing your disabled body staring right back at you. I've experienced it. But you know how the saying goes: 'Your biggest fear carries your largest growth,' and happiness is the most important. There's no rush. It took me some time.

Even if it is day by day or just a few times a month, you'll become much more confident by looking yourself in the eye at the first sight of a mirror every time. I have, and I hope you can do the same someday.

MY LOVE AND HATE RELATIONSHIP USING AUGMENTATIVE AND ALTERNATIVE COMMUNICATION

My brain tells me I'm talking perfectly, but I'm not. Well, my friends often tell me they can sometimes understand me better when I'm under the influence of alcohol. For most people, alcohol makes them slur, but not me. So, I sometimes become the best public speaker in the world. I'm still deciding whether to address the nation, although I could have given Boris Johnson a run for his money. Especially now that he's not Prime Minister anymore.

To help me communicate when people find it difficult to understand me, I use something called augmented and alternative communication. So what is augmented and alternative communication Or AAC, as it's more commonly known. It is a way of communicating that assists or even replaces natural speech. Speech is essential, and it's how we primarily interact and communicate.

So, the first 'A' in AAC represents augmented communication. Augmenting is adding to something or supplementing it. In this case, you can add something to someone's speech, such as sign language, a picture, or a letter board, to get your message across to people. The second 'A' in AAC represents alternative communication, meaning when you cannot speak or be understood by others, like me sometimes.

It gets very frustrating when you are sometimes unable to communicate sufficiently. Trust me, I know. However, different types of AAC can be used to communicate, like unaided ones that don't require someone to use a physical aid. Instead, people may use sign language, facial expressions, body language, or gestures. For example, I may point to something I'm referring to or nod to get my point across.

Then there's aided AAC, which I have used on and off over the years. Aided AAC comes in different forms. For example, some people use symbol boards or sheets, choice cards, communication books, alphabet cards, speech-generating or communication devices, or apps. Until now, I have used text-to-speech AAC systems using a keyboard. But you can get symbol-based AAC. This method is primarily used by people who can't read or spell and use symbols or pictures to represent words or phrases.

HOW I USE MY AAC APP

I started my on-off and love-hate relationship with augmentative and alternative communication in my last year of primary school. I see how AAC software has mostly stayed the same from then until now and how I still use it. The text-to-speech version has virtually the same format and has the same dreary voices. The one positive thing about using AAC is that it allows me to conduct interviews on TV, radio, and podcasts instead of relying on others to speak on my behalf. The only downside to using assistive communication technology for interviews is that they must always be pre-recorded. It takes a lot of time to type into the software. I'm currently using my answers to any questions I may get asked about my books and songwriting exploits.

Nevertheless, I always try to answer every question I get thoroughly. Using AAC is also helpful when I know I need to go somewhere, like the post office or grocery store, and I need to ask for something. Before approaching the customer service assistant, I take myself to one side and type what I need to invite into my AAC app. You are all starting to see a familiar pattern when I use my communication app. Everything needs to be pre-typed or pre-recorded.

However, when using my AAC text-to-speech app for conducting a general everyday conversation, like meeting a group of friends somewhere for a general catch-up, It is just impossible to use because, by the time I have typed in what I wanted to say and joined the conversation, that part of the conversation has finished and moved onto another topic. The fact it's not in real-time is a problem, and that's the part I dislike about using AAC.

So, let's return to my early years and my recollection of using AAC. As with the size of the hardware used, it has become much smaller. It also comes as an app on my iPhone, meaning I now have AAC everywhere. When I first started using it in primary school, it came as a mini laptop called a Lightwriter. The keys on this device were so hard to press that it was horrible. You also had the added burden of carrying this device everywhere, which was exhausting. As you can imagine, AAC has improved significantly in this manner. Moving from a mini-machine to just your mobile phone is much easier.

Using AAC and, when it comes to preserving my identity, even though I have a Welsh accent, well, I hope I have because, to me, I do sound Welsh in my head, It doesn't bother me that I'm not using a Welsh accent on the app because I want to have a way to communicate the important things that I need and want to be able to say. I always try to express my true feelings and personality when I use my AAC app, and the odd joke or a funny one-liner usually breaks the ice in most conversations. If I had any advice for people using it, especially younger people, never be embarrassed to use it. As I have just explained, it has taken me years to realise that using AAC has some advantages, like helping non-verbal people and people like me who have speech impediments to communicate in an accessible way that allows both themselves and others around them to converse well.

Grab these advantages with both hands and make the most of them. Even though using AAC isn't the quickest and most cutting-edge technology yet, its advancement may be just around the corner. Who knows what lies ahead? I don't know what's waiting around the corner, but I need to type faster to use AAC and drink alcohol more often to talk clearly. Even then, stranger things have and can happen! It's good to talk!

SPEECH AND LANGUAGE THERAPIST

If this makes sense, I am trying to turn my love-hate relationship into more of a love-love relationship. Now, I am still growing in confidence when attending networking events, author events, or book signings, and I have to speak more publicly. Whether it's introducing myself at networking events or conducting author talks, everything is pre-recorded, and I check in with any questions or what I need to discuss. So, after not seeing one for the last thirty years, I decided to consult with a speech and language therapist.

When I was writing this book, I had already attended some consultations. For those who have never heard of a speech and language therapist and are wondering what they do, They provide treatment and support for children and adults with difficulty communicating, drinking, or swallowing. Admittedly, going back and seeing a speech and language therapist after all those years did make me a little anxious. Once again, overthinking Gavin emerged.

But once I got to the consultation room and started talking with my speech and language therapist, they put me at ease. I asked if it was normal for my speech to sound as if it were normal in my head, but it was not being spoken commonly, and they reassured me that this was very common and nothing to worry about. They also confirmed that having a speech therapy programme in my case wouldn't improve my speech tremendously, and the little progress I would make would take me a long time to master. Remember, everybody has the desire and right to be able to speak for themselves. However, I understand that this may not be possible for some people, even with the help of augmentative and alternative communication aids.

INACCESSIBLE WORLD

Using AAC can give people the desired voice and even change their lives. However, AAC may be more complex, practical, and conventional. But this may be the only way to express themselves and portray their beliefs. So please take a moment and put yourself in their shoes, be kind, and make extra time to communicate with them and listen to them because what they may have to say could change how you view the world forever.

Being disabled often leads to challenges in navigating our unforgiving and inaccessible world. It becomes so frustrating when an inaccessible venue or a speech impediment stops you from progressing, helping you on your way to success, not attending a job interview for a role you set your heart on, or going on a night out with friends. In the past, I have refrained from attending an author or songwriting networking event alone due to worrying about nobody understanding my speech. Attending unfamiliar events makes me somewhat anxious now.

Thoughts run through my head, like, Will the event be easily accessible? Where can I sit down and rest my legs for a bit? Will people try to avoid interacting with me because they can't understand what I'm saying? But strangely, over time, something inside me made me still turn up and be seen. The older I get, the more determined and resilient I'm getting to show people that my physical difference and my speech impediment aren't the barriers stopping me from following my dreams. It's the inaccessibility and outdated societal attitudes that are stopping it.

I believe disability representation within our society is vital, and the way we can help and improve the visibility of disabled people in our everyday lives is to remove the many societal barriers and ableist attitudes disabled people face once and for all. We can further accelerate this vital process by ensuring that people in charge of disability, like the standing Minister of Parliament or State for Disabled People, Health, and Work, unite with their devolved counterparts here in the UK and adopt a one-nation multifaceted approach to providing much more support through education, using our media and social media platforms to promote disability awareness and disability rights, Only then can we strengthen our advocacy to get changes in our laws and policies looked at and put in place. Leading to better overall accessibility, changing societal attitudes, and changing past negative stereotypes, then putting inclusion and disability diversity at the forefront of society, which will ease the fears of doing wrong by the people who essentially are the inspiration and educational cogs for generations to come.

MY AMBITION AND JEALOUSY

For me, fearing the unknown has played a significant role in me being sceptical occasionally, and this scepticism has made me feel so frustrated because I know that if it weren't for my disabilities, there's so much more I might have been able to achieve in my life. I'm very ambitious, sometimes impulsive, and want to be the best person I can be. You often try too hard, mainly because you want to prove that despite physical disabilities, you want to do the things that non-disabled people sometimes can do more easily than you can. I admit that my frustration has made me jealous of non-disabled people because they have achieved more than I could have, and this frustration and jealousy combined have affected my mental health at various stages of my life. If it wasn't for my parents, who helped me manage my expectations and pushed me to achieve my dreams, I'm not sure what unnecessary harm I could have done to my body.

Over the years, there have been many arguments I have had with my parents about putting the brakes on my high expectations. But deep down, I have always known they have had to be tough when managing my ego for my well-being, mental health, and life. So my advice for parents with disabled children is that even though they too may be sceptical about how capable their child will end up being as they navigate through what is still a very inaccessible world for disabled people, and even though I have previously said that letting your disabled child fly in this life and reach for the stars is sometimes the best way for them to find their feet, Sometimes, you may need to clip their wings a little and even be there for them when frustration, sadness, or depression sets in. Because when you are at your lowest, the first people you turn to are your parents, who have always supported you no matter what. Just being there will always be enough.

CHAPTER 9
THE MISUNDERSTOOD MAN

"Every life holds value, regardless of location, age, gender or disability. There is a plan and a purpose for every one" – **Sharron Angle**

Most of the time, I'm full of life and the soul of the party. I often come up with funny one-liners, although sometimes people don't understand what I say. I'm a mixture of Dara O'Brian and The Lost Voice Guy morphed into one person. Still, people laugh anyway. Well, at least, I think they do.

It's challenging to be happy all the time. When you are different, you stand out from the crowd. There are some theories that humans are similar to group-living animals. We tend to herd spontaneously. We often stick to our preferred groups and routines and are reluctant to change. We like seeing ourselves as similar to others, which is why most people outside your social circle are different from the stereotypical group members you are used to interacting with. We become frightened, rebel, naturally become protective of the norm, and fight against change in specific ways. We may lash out, become physical, use horrible language to vent and protect, and sometimes block out parts of society we fear or dislike as a protection mechanism.

People often say, 'well, it's not our fault we rebel against different things. It's how we are wired.' So, let's stop for a minute. If we were all wired the same, would we all look the same, act the same, eat the same, and even maybe poo at the same time? I'm sorry, but stupid comments like these are unacceptable. We are herd-group-living humans. Yes, I get that. Still, this doesn't mean we always have to follow the stereotype and let fear take over. The brain is a very complex organ that plays an astronomical role in controlling not only the muscles throughout our bodies but also our emotions. It controls how you think and, most notably, how you act.

BREAKING NEWS (Well, not exclusively breaking news, but I'll say it anyway).

WE ALL HAVE OUR OWN BRAINS AND THE ABILITY TO CHOOSE HOW WE ACT AND WHAT WE DO FOR OURSELVES!

Believe it or not, yes, we can strive to make the right and moral decisions. Even non-verbal people want to massively contribute to what's going on in the world around them. They need to do it differently. How you act can determine how you feel at any given time and how others think, too. There's a saying, 'there's a time and place in this world for everyone.' Most of the time, our actions speak louder and do more than words can. So, treating a disabled person as you treat everyone else can instantly make them feel included.

Some people are extroverts, others are introverts, and interacting can be challenging. Still, when someone has the awareness that disabled people are humans, that speaks volumes. They become the ones who educate. Essentially, they become a herd leader who teaches the value of respect and shows the others in the pack how to be respectful.

So, hopefully, you can now get my point. Respectable values teach others moral values, and having more disability awareness and representation within society teaches people about disability and its associated barriers. Then, once we get enough disability awareness and not only the voices of disability advocates but also their allies are listened to respectfully and entirely, societal attitudes can change for the better.

MY DOS AND DON'TS

So, now I'd like to talk about and explain my beliefs and my pet hates. The dos and don'ts when it comes to interacting with disabled people we are all our own people. We all have routines and specific traits and values instilled in our identities. Still, we all forget that our values may not be acceptable to others and could exclude them. How we act or go about our daily routines can harm people, including disabled people, and sometimes, we don't realise we are disrespectful.

I'm at the age now where I am becoming more knowledgeable, except for the odd crazy moments like falling over drunk and breaking my ribs. I have more life experience, 'I think'. Therefore, I am becoming more comfortable in my skin, which is good. You concentrate on the more simple things in your life, like family and friends, and wonder how often you will have to go to the toilet through the night as you grow older. It comes to us all eventually. Still, it comes with age for most people. You stop caring so much about what other people think of you, and that peer pressure from your younger years that you've let hang around fades away.

Although I've been out and about, there have been times when I haven't felt good, and that feeling of internal ableism comes rushing to me. Those negative thoughts and self-doubt have taken over. Still, generally, after a good night's sleep and with my mother or father giving me a good talk, shaking me down, and telling me to be proud of my inner qualities, followed by a 'that's my boy', I'm back to being my determined old self and ready to fight the world again. On this note, I want to assure you. It's perfectly normal to feel like you are not worthy or good enough. As disabled people, we allow ourselves to overthink too much, and thoughts like 'what would my life be like if I was non-disabled?' are perfectly fine, and it's justifiable to think this way because I have done it in the past and still do.

Being asked in the past if I had ever thought about what my life would be like if I wasn't disabled is one of the most challenging questions I've had to answer. A friend asked. His words were met with audible gasps from the people we were hanging out with.

"Have you ever thought about what your life would be like if you weren't disabled?"

But there was no need for them to be nervous; I'm at an age now where I know that answering these questions helps educate others. It took me a few seconds to think about my answer, but I answered yes. I now realise more than ever that you can't change the person you are. We are all unique in our ways, and now, as much as I wouldn't want to be disabled, I am. This is who I am. I am proud of myself and my achievements.

I JUST WANT TO BE SEEN AS 'ONE OF THE BOYS.

I have sometimes gone over what it would be like not to be disabled. Sometimes, I didn't want to see or label myself as disabled. I wanted to be 'one of the boys'. I wish I had known then that being disabled doesn't mean that can't happen. It's a heartbreaking and horrible feeling to be left out because of what your body can and can't do, but unfortunately, to accept yourself as a disabled person, you have to come to terms with this, too. For me, this realisation came with time and my body telling me I physically couldn't keep up when my brain was telling me I could.

I've had time to do a bit of soul-searching and reflect on my life. I am proud of my accomplishments until now, and I'm still working on achieving, inspiring, and breaking through many barriers. But I have done well in life, so I no longer need to ask myself 'what if'? I am who I am; my friends and family have always seen me that way. They have loved and accepted me as disabled from day one. They've never wished I were anyone different, so why should I?

Over the years, there have been certain things I have had to learn to deal with. There were other people staring at me. Now I know that my walk is acceptably different from others, and probably that children will stare, which is understandable. However, I am happy for them to stare as much as they want because I know they are inquisitive. For example, they ask their parents why they might walk differently, leading them to have an educational family discussion. But when adults blatantly stare, I find the situation awkward and ignorant. I don't know how to act.

DON'T STARE! IT'S RUDE!

I have been out with friends socialising on a night out, and when the drinks start flowing, I have endured the odd remark from someone walking by, purely to make them feel like 'the big guy' in their circle of friends. Still, I have great friends who always have my back and never stand for or tolerate that kind of behaviour, and they stick up for me or even sometimes stop me from confronting these uneducated people. They are not worth the energy or time. With the widely available amount of ever-growing educational material and diversity, people should be more socially responsible for their and their friends' actions. Remember that it is perfectly 'OK' to be accepting of others, especially of those who are a bit different. These uncalled-for remarks could affect that disabled person deep down, causing their internal ableism to flare up.

So please, while I am now talking about people blatantly staring, I hope I have brought this to your attention, and maybe you are thinking to yourself, 'I have done this in the past.' I genuinely believe that 99% of the time, people find themselves staring at disabled people unconsciously. After all, as humans, we are inquisitive, and it's in our nature to react this way when confronted with something unfamiliar or different from our daily experiences. Still, I know from experience that it can be uncomfortable for the person being stared at. Still, I have tried to bring this to everyone's attention. It's important to remember, whether we are disabled or not, that everyone deserves respect and personal space, no matter their physical appearance or differences.

SOCIALISING WITH A DISABILITY AND WHAT HAVING ACCESS TO SOCIETY MEANS TO ME

An active social life has been essential to who I have become. My parents were determined to set me on the best path possible. So, as a child, they included me in as many activities as my disability allowed me to undertake. As a result, my social life has been full-on, and I am forever grateful to my parents for showing me, 'let us say, the Welsh way, the fun way, the happy way.' Admittedly, I have partied as hard as my body physically allowed me to until now and beyond. Although my body is telling me to slow down, my brain is still in party mode sometimes, but you know what they say, 'work hard and play even harder.'

As mentioned above, my family and friends have never left me out and have included me in every social event they organise. Whether it's birthday parties, stag parties, football tours, or even a lad's trip abroad, if I am physically able and well enough to attend any event, I will attend. I rarely miss out on a good old knees-up. Without my parents' will and encouragement, I couldn't have achieved such an independent social life. They wanted me to get out there. They wanted me to show the world who I am and that my disabilities are only a tiny part of who I am. 'It's all about your personality and being kind and accepting of people for who they are, not about their appearance. 'You must never judge a book by its cover.' So my mum always tells me, even now.

We need to stop being so judgemental as a society. Just because somebody doesn't fit in or stand up to your stereotype doesn't mean they are not worthy of achieving, socialising, loving someone, being loved back, or even partying until sunrise. If they want to live their best life or follow their dreams, they should become a politician, an author, or even a music mogul. They deserve the right to take their chance at becoming successful.

There is no such thing as "NORMAL." Nobody's perfect. We all make mistakes, and through my past experiences, I know we become stronger and wiser by making mistakes. But, remember, underneath our skin, we are all the same, apart from the odd broken bone, lung puncture, kidney failure, and so on. You get what I mean. We all come into this world naked and go out of it naked. I will be anyway, Starkers.

In the past, I have used a wheelchair to get around, especially on trips where there has been a lot of walking, and I must admit I am stubborn and will walk a little until I am physically tired and my legs hurt. One reason is that sometimes, in the past, I did not want to become a burden to my friends and family. I now know that being in a wheelchair does not make you a burden. It is the barriers around us that do that. Or, in my case, how I don't want to be perceived by the world. Inclusion and acceptance are essential; access to an active social life is vital to creating a more inclusive world. I get that people have different disabilities, and the severity may mean you cannot get around or go out. Still, everybody has a right to a social life if they choose to have one, whether they are non-disabled, have a physical disability, have a learning disability, or have a hidden disability.

WE NEED MORE ACCESSIBLE VENUES

There is nothing more upsetting than going to a concert or venue after all the planning and excitement and being turned away because the place where it is situated or the building where the function or concert is happening is not accessible because you are either in a wheelchair or because it is too far away or difficult to get there by foot. I am so independent, but some people may need assistance regarding socialising. There is nothing wrong with a disabled person going on a well-deserved shopping trip, a meal, a friendly drink with friends, or even a holiday with a carer, or as people prefer to call them today, a personal assistant. However, to become more socially inclusive, we need to zone in from a positive and collaborative perspective and think about ways to make our lives much more accessible, such as our pavements and pathways, parks, and green spaces, especially our hospitality spaces and venues.

For example, when visiting nightlife venues with friends, I have had to assess the situation upon arrival and sometimes go to a different venue than everybody else with somebody willing to accompany me. I get anxious about tripping over because of the other venue, where everybody else is, after seeing the number of steps or different heights off the floor. Whereas with a bit of initiative by that particular venue, maybe, if possible and practical within the venue's layout, installing accessible aids such as lifts, more even ramps, walkways, and handrails, I could have joined everyone at the preferred venue. To others, this may come across as a little pessimistic. Still, for someone with a disability, who has limited mobility, or who uses a wheelchair, these significant changes could be the difference between becoming more included at more venues or being left out or left behind altogether. These adjustments make a difference. Being more mindful of this will make my night out and many other people's nights out all that more memorable.

Yes, each venue has differences and limitations on how we can make them more accessible. Some buildings and spaces are many years old. Still, this does not mean we cannot become more accessible-minded, get more accessibility aids into venues, train staff on dealing with different types of disabilities, and interact with different spectrums and scales of disability.

Then, we move on to music, putting on sensory and movement events for deaf and blind people. Admittedly, these few elements I have touched upon are just a few adjustments we can make. By any means, I am no expert on how to make our venues accessible, and I can only give my personal feelings on this subject. 'Everybody deserves access to an active social life, no matter what.' It's time we all come together, take action, and indefinitely make our society accessible for everyone.

REPRESENTATION OF DISABILITIES IN THE MEDIA AND BROADER COMMUNITY

There's a secret weapon to help us advocate for and represent the disabled community; we must utilise this more. Please wait for it, and it's on our media, TV screens, and social media.

Even though disability sports were only becoming recognised all those years ago, I was so stubborn and determined to be with my friends that I chose not to pursue them. The way disability sports have progressed these days It is getting much better. You only need to look at the Paralympics' growth and worldwide brand. Still, there's a 'but' coming. We need more disability sports and disabilities represented in the mainstream media and integrated and shown more in our communities.

Look at women's football and how it is slowly progressing into a more professional and covered sport. Years ago, you had never heard of women's football. Now, it's getting prime-time television coverage. So, my thoughts and hopes are why can't disabled football get more funds and become a professional sport represented in the media? We are far from this becoming a reality, but it is not impossible.

We also must start moving towards having more disabled actors become more included and seen in leading and educational roles on our screens. By this, I mean disabled actors playing disabled roles, including people with physical disabilities, learning disabilities, and even hidden ones. The more representation we have in the media, the more not only today's generation will learn about disability, but future generations will, too. Educating on the positive ways disabled people can thrive is vital, and the media can be the driving force behind it and help us become more inclusive.

Representation is improving, but a lot more needs to be done. Only then can we make significant strides in this direction so society can learn how to adopt a more open and inclusive mindset.

I was overwhelmed and happy to see Tommy Jessop play Terry Boyle's role in the drama Line of Duty. It was such a powerful storyline that highlighted that the exploitation of disabled people does happen. The role played by an actor with Down syndrome is a massive achievement and a big step in the right direction. Let's hope this opens the floodgates for more disabled people to play significant roles on our screens. We also must remember Rosie Jones, a comedian with cerebral palsy who is currently getting many mainstream TV roles and appearances. Also, not forgetting The Lost Voice Guy Lee Ridley and his sitcom 'Ability', which he co-wrote and starred in, again, let's hope that these disabled roles on our TV screens become a lot more frequent.

HOW DO YOU INTERACT WITH PEOPLE WITH ALL KINDS OF DISABILITIES?

The answer to this is straightforward. Treat disabled people the same as everyone else. That way, you are a lot more inclusive and friendly. I have already touched on this subject. Unfortunately, in the past and in some instances, I have been spoken to as if I cannot interact confidently with whoever I am conversing with. It is as if people think I am still a child, and that person starts to engage with me more slowly and demeaningly. It is as if they believe I am a robot. Whenever this happens, a streak of unease and bewilderment thunderbolts through my body and deep down into my soul while I think to myself.

'Why does this person think I'm incapable of interacting with them confidently like anyone else?'

I was born with cerebral palsy and a speech impediment, meaning I suffered a brain injury at birth, which is why I have physical and neurological disabilities. Still, having these disabilities doesn't define me or how I go about my academic life or interact with others. I understand that there are many different types of disabilities that affect people in many ways. Some people may need more help and assistance, but being different doesn't mean you are less able in other ways, such as academically. It just means that sometimes you may need to do certain things differently from others or take a little longer to do some activities. Stephen Hawkin is a fine example. He was one of the most knowledgeable people in the world. He never let his disabilities stop him from studying at Oxford University, where he received his first-class BA degree in physics, which later meant he became one of the most well-known physicists in the world. His disabilities never stopped him from achieving what he did.

THE HISTORY OF DISABILITY AND HOW FAR WE'VE COME

History suggests that being disabled many years ago was not that great. Research indicates that as far back as the early 1900s, disabled people were segregated from society, and little was known about the social, scientific, and medical conditions surrounding the many kinds of disabilities. Fast-forward to today, and we live in a much more knowledgeable world. We have a better understanding of the many disabilities that exist. Medically, treatments are vastly improving, allowing people with disabilities to live more independently and longer.

Every disabled person is different regarding assistance and

how they get on with their lives. Whether it's with the provision of disability aids or needing a little personal help from time to time, service providers will have undoubtedly made past mistakes, under-cared for people, misled people, and underperformed. But we can all learn from the past. Suppose we, the disabled person, are able and willing. In that case, we can educate the government, local authorities, and the public on how we live our lives independently and more inclusively. We can make the future a better place for everyone by being consulted on how society can become more inclusive. After all, we are best placed to advise on how to make these much-needed changes. Starting with making our society, venues, and outside spaces easily accessible for everyone by ensuring access to areas and amenities such as public toilets, retail outlets, and hospitality are at the forefront of our immediate and future regeneration projects Then, by doing this, we can start turning our beautiful world into an inclusive one. Of course, we still have some way to go on this. Still, with the right mindset and consultation with disabled people, we can make huge strides and create a more inclusive and happy future.

LEARNING TO DRIVE

For years, I have had many mixed reactions in situations where people have asked how I travelled to an event or venue. They ask questions or say, 'Oh, it must have taken you ages to travel here by public transport.' Or, 'If your parents have dropped you here, they don't need to wait. We can call them to pick you up or drop you home when we finish.' People automatically assume I cannot drive because of a physical difference in appearance. Again, ableist stereotypes rush into people's mindsets, and when I tell them that I've driven my car to the required location, they sometimes look at me as if I have two heads. Which still saddens me. Still, many more disabled people are learning to drive for many reasons, including that the vehicles we drive now are getting so advanced that at the push of a button, you can start an engine.

I passed my test when I was twenty-one. Incredibly, and to my sheer surprise, I passed the first time. I learned to drive with the British School of Motoring and had weekly Sunday morning lessons for the better part of the year. I learned to drive an automatic car and still have only driven automated-geared vehicles because the left side of my body is my strongest and I experience most of the stiffness in my right arm. To be honest, I often forget that my right arm is attached to my body. I rarely use it. Also, to assist people who have physical differences with driving, many gadgets and adaptations have been invented, designed, and are now fitted to cars that disabled people drive.

I use a left-foot accelerator as opposed to a right-foot one! I also have a left-sided steering wheel handle with a 10-way infrared steering wheel control, where I can operate my indicators, wipers, lights, screen wash, and horn at the press of a button. So, if you have a disability and are pondering learning to drive, give it serious consideration. I know every disability is different, but learning to drive and passing my test have been life-changing. It's given me independence and a social life.

Charitable schemes are available where disabled people can get help, advice, and even funding by leasing a car from specialist car dealers. Furthermore, they can be assessed and have their vehicles specially adapted to suit their disabilities. It then makes it easier for them to drive. For example, I use the Motability Scheme, which is widely available through many mainstream car dealers around the UK.

Learning to drive and passing my test have been life-changing, and I would urge every young disabled person who doubts whether they'll be able to drive to get some advice and get out there on the road. It has given me my independence and meant that I haven't had to rely on family and friends when getting around. Trust me; I'm stubborn, and if I want to do something or go somewhere, try to stop me. So I grab my car keys, and off I go. But being able to control my independence means the world. It means that at any given time, I can attend appointments and meetings, go shopping, pop out to catch up with friends, get myself to songwriting studio sessions, and attend author events and book signings.

MY BLUE DISABLED BADGE

I also have a UK Blue Disabled Parking Permit, or a Blue Disabled Badge, as they are more commonly known. It permits me, as a disabled driver and vehicle owner, special privileges to park in disabled parking bays, on yellow lines, or in a time-limited parking area, and sometimes park in a metre-controlled car park free of charge. This gives me more room to manoeuvre out of my car, or if I use a wheelchair, more space to get in and out of the wheelchair in my vehicle, or vice versa. Disabled parking bays also allow disabled people to get better, more accessible, and safer access to venues like hospitals, medical centres, shopping centres, cinemas, theatres, and most hospitality and retail spaces and areas nationwide. Most disabled people use the Blue Disabled Parking Permit. So even if you don't drive and someone drives for you, you are still entitled to get one.

In the UK, older people are entitled to a blue disabled parking permit. Let's face it: almost everyone becomes less mobile due to bone wear and tear or arthritis. These creep upon us before we know it or before we can say, 'Bob's your uncle." It's all part of growing old. So, we deserve a few entitlements as we age. Still, throughout the last twenty years of my life, ever since I passed my test, I, like my family, did so before I got my road independence and have continued to use my Blue Disabled Parking Badge. I admit I am younger than some others who use disabled parking badges. Still, I am legally entitled to use one.

There are sometimes misconceptions around these entitlements, though, and many people may use the Blue Disabled Parking Badge, including not only people with physical disabilities but also those with hidden disabilities such as autism and their personal assistants, along with cancer treatment patients. I nearly always use my Blue Disabled Parking

Permit due to my limited mobility, and my limited mobility is visible. Still, there are occasions where I have been questioned, stared at, and even confronted by other people for using disabled parking bays, and it still baffles me to some extent. I don't know whether it has been because of my age or the types of cars I have driven, but I still get questioned and stared at today.

I also get frustrated when I see non-disabled people parking in disabled parking bays and when they get confronted about why they've parked there when they don't have a blue badge. The most common excuse I hear is, 'oh, I'll only be a minute. Well, I'm sorry, but that minute is too long. What if a wheelchair user or someone with limited mobility needs to get to a one-time urgent appointment and needs an easy access route or more space to set their wheelchair up? You are stopping them from making their appointment on time. So think before you park.

MY DISABLED PARKING BAY IDEA

I often wonder why they haven't made disabled parking bays with attached electronic tags or recognition systems. So, for instance, somewhere on your car's window, you get to secure a sensor that holds all of your blue parking badge details, and then every disabled parking bay gets fitted with a tag or sensor reader that reads your badge's details in your window. Suppose the information stored within your sensor corresponds with centralised local authority databases. In that case, you are entitled to park with the sensor in the parking bay going green, letting everyone else know you are entitled to park there. Alternatively, if you don't have a blue parking sensor and are naughty parking in those bays without any consideration for disabled people, the disabled parking bay's tag or sensor will stay red; you get a small fine if you aren't moved after a period. After that, the money they generate could be used to help our venues become more accessible and to help pay for more complex things, such as adaptations to disabled people's houses so they can live in a safer environment.

Another good idea is to separate disabled parking bays into two categories: ones for disabled people, especially wheelchair users, and ones for low-mobility people or older adults. Disabled people are outnumbered and sometimes find it challenging to locate a suitable bay. Some bays are a lot less comprehensive than others. Remember, wheelchair users usually need more manoeuvring space than, for example, an older adult.

Please, can I ask you to embrace the #bekind movement regarding using disabled parking bays? So many people are entitled to use them, so can I ask people to look at people who park in them with a non-judgemental mindset because you never know what people are dealing with at that moment?

One last piece of advice I want to help you with is if you are in a position where you think you may need to use a blue disabled parking permit. Most local councils deal with issuing them nowadays. Some allow you to apply for them traditionally by filling out application forms, which you call your regional council offices to get. Still, in this day and age, most local councils only deal with online applications, so it may be worth Googling how to acquire a permit locally.

STOP ASKING WHERE MY CARER IS WHEN I'M GOING ABOUT MINDING MY OWN BUSINESS.

Ultimately, as a nation, most of us are compassionate and caring. It's in our nature. Respect is something most of us value and something that makes us want to look out for and care for the vulnerable and disabled, including me. It would be a worrying trait if vulnerable people were left to fend for themselves instead of being cared for, upholding their human rights and dignity. Anyone with a genuinely caring soul instinctively wants to be able to care for others, especially their loved ones.

There are times when I need help being cared for. With a physical disability, undoubtedly, as I get older, this care and support will become more of a regular thing. My disabilities could inevitably get worse, meaning more help will be needed.

At the time of writing this book, I am still able to mainly care for myself and get around adequately without continuous assistance. Despite this, random people occasionally approach me, asking where my carer or personal assistant is. With the utmost respect, I'm fortunate enough not to need full-time assistance at this stage. For now, at least, my mother helps me with some essential everyday chores and activities. Please be aware of and acknowledge that my friends are exactly that. They are people who I have grown up with for many years, not my carers.

I get strangers stopping me in the street and asking, 'Excuse me, where's your carer?'

Their reaction when I reply that I don't have one is usually a mixture of amazement and disgust. It feels like they are on a power trip, and seeing somebody different getting on with their own life independently worries them. But there is no need. I understand that, on some occasions, these members of the public are well-meaning. But I am a grown man with feelings and a soul, and I like to keep my head high. While some people are genuinely kind, I'm not a child, and when they ask where my carer is, it feels as though they assume that I am incapable of being within the community on my own.

There have been times when people have been forceful to the point where they have actively manhandled me without asking me if I need assistance. Each disability is different, and mine is a physical one. It has taken me a while to reach this point in my life where I can, to a certain point, manage my disabilities alone. Having cerebral palsy does hold me back a little. Still, I have realised that getting on with everyday life at a slower pace is better than being unable to be as independent as I am, and independence means everything to me. I would have hoped that attitudes around disability had changed and that more people would know that it is unacceptable to approach someone and assume you know better than they do about how they should live their life. However, the world we live in is getting savvier, medicine and science are getting more advanced, and technology has come on leaps and bounds. All this helps disabled people live much better and longer lives.

It knocks my confidence when people assume I need a full-time carer or personal assistant. It makes me feel like they think I have no right to be independent because I don't fit their stereotype of what people should be like. It's heartbreaking, and these attitudes need to change. I want to ask people to remember that asking a disabled person why their carer is rude and derogatory can be rude and demeaning. It implies that I am a societal hazard and should be cared for. It makes me so angry that people still see disabled people as second-class citizens and, sometimes, as a burden to society.

STOP INFANTILIZING ME AND OTHER DISABLED PEOPLE.

All through my life and up until this stage, I have sometimes been infantilized, which still happens. It wasn't until recently that someone brought to my attention that this continues because I tend to retract into myself while talking to certain people. I'm not sure if it's a habit I've developed to cope with having a disability or a way of protecting myself, but it's my fault it happens, and I need to get brave.

Infantilizing someone is when you treat them as a child or in a way that undermines or denies their maturity, age, achievements, or experience. Typical infantilizing behaviour may be how people act towards someone, interact with someone, or speak to someone. But, look, I'm now a grown adult and not a child, and I'm not a lap dog or anyone's pet. So stop infantilizing me.

Yes, I am different from society's stereotypical normal, which makes me stand out. I tell people about what it's like to live with cerebral palsy and the barriers disabled people deal with every day. I do this because I want to make a difference and show both the generations of today and tomorrow that having a disability doesn't mean you can't live the way you want and become successful. Do I want to be a role model and an inspiration? Of course I do. But I want to inspire people by using creativity and education, so people and the wider society can strive to become more inclusive for everyone. So, to be clear, I haven't become The Disabled Writer just for pity. I have done so because I want to make a difference, push for change in attitudes by using bold statements, continue to follow my dreams, and try to succeed like any other determined person, whether disabled or not. Ok, secretly, I would like to become a millionaire and travel the world, but most of us have those aspirations.

Over the years, I now know that, unconsciously, I have fallen into the trap of being susceptible to becoming infantilized and saving the hassle of causing a scene by calling people out for doing it. But I am now in my forties. I can make my own decisions and need to start confidently owning my actions. I may need help with difficult things, like cooking or ironing. Still, I am not a child, so please don't talk to me like one.

PLEASE, TALK TO ME!

I visited Benidorm with a friend. After three years of restrictions and lockdowns, it was lovely to have a breakaway, and I thoroughly enjoyed our holiday. But, while I was out and about, exploring, partying, and having a good time, I noticed that something was happening, which repeatedly made me feel anxious. I felt like I was being ignored, even bypassed, when interacting and conversing with other holidaymakers because I have cerebral palsy and a speech impediment. Because of this, I became increasingly aware that some people would speak to my friend about something they wanted to know about me or ask them a question on my behalf as if they thought or implied I wasn't able to or educated enough to reply. I wonder if I'm older and wiser, so I am noticing this happening more and more. Now, I am progressing into my, let's say, 'limelight years' and into my forties. I am becoming more confident in my skin, and I now have enough life experience that I do want to answer any difficult questions about my disabilities that people want to know.

I get curious people who want to ask questions about my disabilities. I love that people care and are interested enough to ask because this is how they learn how different disabilities affect different people. Then they understand how we live our lives and sometimes realise that you can still live an active and sociable life to the best of your abilities if your disabilities allow you to. Despite having cerebral palsy, I am still mobile and functional. Still, I respect that other disabled people may not be able to get around as well as I can. Therefore, I will always try to answer every disability question. But please, can I ask people when they are speaking to me or want to ask me a question? Ask me directly first because I find it very infantilizing and demoralising when people assume I am not educated or academically focused enough to answer questions for myself and interact directly with my friends in the first instance. I wouldn't have already written and had three books published if I was incapable and unsure of my capabilities.

I'M A HUMAN, JUST LIKE YOU

Disabled people are human beings the same as everyone else, even if they look different, don't fit into past stereotypes, or are not communicating in a way that you are used to. Disabled people have a soul and want to feel and be included like the rest of society. So, in general, please stop talking to or about disabled people in the third person or as if they are an object and making an instant assumption about that person. If you are going to ask them a question, ask them directly. Stop directing questions to the person or people with them and wait to speak to their partner, friend, personal assistant, or BSL interpreter. Instead, ask them the question directly in the first instance; if they don't feel confident enough to answer you, they'll ask for help.

Here's an example: Start by asking a disabled person a direct question like, 'What is YOUR favourite colour?' instead of using the third person and non-inclusive language, 'What is THEIR favourite colour?' Then, if they feel confident enough to answer you immediately, you will know where you can take the conversation directly or indirectly. If they decide to bring in another person to help, please respect that the conversation may end up being a mixture of first person, direct dialogue with them, and third person, where the other person will help you and the disabled person communicate efficiently.

As I have written in this book, disabled people sometimes use other communication methods. For example, augmentative and alternative communication, sometimes with Eyegaze technology some AAC users may use head pointers or hands-free mouses. Others may use switches to access their devices. However, using some communication aids is not too conventional and can be time-consuming. Still, they allow disabled people to have the ability to communicate within society. In addition, they are a form of outlet; they allow people with speech impediments or who are non-verbal to be heard.

I get that there will continue to be instances where people are unwilling to educate themselves on the different scales of disability before interacting or making a judgement, as well as stereotypes. But unfortunately, these oversimplified images of people will always be in our society.

Despite my experiences, I believe that through education

in our schools and on social media, we can start to educate the broader society on how to interact with all kinds of disabled people through more disability awareness programmes in our workplaces, retail, tourism, and hospitality sectors. But our government, devolved governments, and local authorities need to liaise with the disabled community on a larger scale to achieve this. Primarily, disabled people are the ones who live through these experiences and, therefore, are the best people to advise on how we can make our society a more inclusive one.

Please be kind when speaking with or asking a disabled person a question. Ask them directly in the first instance because you never know how knowledgeable these people could be, and they will most likely inspire you for the rest of your life in an educational way. Never make a judgement before really getting to know someone, especially when you first meet people with disabilities, because not every disability is associated with learning disabilities or mental illness. These people have feelings, emotions, and aspirations just as non-disabled people do, and rightly so.

Taking Part In A Charity Single At Shabbey Road Studios.

In The Studio With Forces Sweetheart, Kirsten Osborne.

With Al Steele And Darren In The Studio.

Listening To A Song Mix In The Studio.

In The Studio With Peter Karrie, Phantom Of The Opera.

Standing At The Podium In The Senedd.

With My Publisher, Clare, Katherine And Lyndon Of Sudol Media, On Our Visit To The Senedd.

Here I am: my books, Max and the Magic Wish and Paddy the Polar Bear Teddy.

Attending A Book Fair In Newport Riverfront Theatre With My Children's Books Max and Paddy.

Ever The Joker.

Taking part in a fundraiser
to raise money for Cerebral Palsy Cymru.

Meeting Warren Gatland At A Rugby Events Evening.

Welsh Rugby Legend, Shane Williams.

One Of The Many Tours I Went On With Great Friends.

With My Mum.

With my sister-in-law, Charlotte.

With Music Producer Al Steele Outside Shabbey Road Studios.

CHAPTER 10
THE JOKER

"Being disabled means taking a slightly different path, but it doesn't hinder our potential." —**Robert M, Hensel**

As you've probably figured out from reading the last nine chapters, I am slightly crazy and a joker. I've gotten myself out of a few sticky situations and blagged my way into some pleasant situations because I'm disabled. I will continue to do so until society becomes more accessible and inclusive. As a disabled person, some people question your mentality as if they still see you as a kid or expect you not to be able to be adultlike. Therefore, my defence mechanism for coping with this ignorance is to play along and get away with stuff most people wouldn't do, and anyone can play that game, whether disabled or not.

I'm relatively quick-witted, and as for banter, I can give as good as possible if there is miscommunication due to my speech impediment. I let my actions or even bold, funny statements do the talking. Still, I want to stress that a line must not be crossed, and we must respect other people's dignity and feelings, disabilities or not!

This chapter, even though it's short and witty, You know what they say, 'If you can't convince them, confuse the pants out of them.' That is what I do anyway. I will let you all in on some of the funny, silly, sarcastic, and drunken things I have done so far throughout my chaotic life. So, here it goes.

FUNNY SLOGANS, SMALL TALK, AND SELLING LAND ROVERS AMONG OTHER ANTICS

Laughter is the best way to break the ice in any situation, whether on a night out or in the workplace. They say it's the best form of medicine. Going back to when I was in my twenties and my prime partying years, let's say I wanted to enjoy life. Well, let's say I wanted to live life in the fast lane too. Even though my internal ableism can strike upon my soul at any time, one of my most prevalent thoughts and mottos is, 'we are only here in this world once. Life is for living, so bloody live it.'

I enjoy being the joker. Still, on some occasions, some people can get offended. However, I have known great friends for many years, and the banter we have between each other is excellent. We know how to make each other laugh; we take the mickey out of one another, and I give out as much as I get back. Still, we respect other people and know how many buttons we can push within the limits of our banter.

There have been times, though, when people have been offended by how much banter there is between us and taken offence because of my disabilities. They'll say, 'You are being offensive to him. He's disabled.' I get where people are coming from and may genuinely see what's going on as being offensive towards me, but on the other hand, what they don't see is that I do have limits, and my close friends know this, and they or I wouldn't let random people insult me in any way. My disabilities are physical, not learning or mental. I know when people are crossing the line, and I will speak out whenever I feel it's been crossed.

I can defend myself, and I will always endeavour to champion disability rights. Still, it would help if you always had time to find a balance and a breaking point where you must enjoy life, too. Admittedly, this balance is difficult to sustain because there are so many different disabilities and stereotypes associated with them. So instinctively, people become overprotective of other people, but on the flip side of this coin, disabled people are entitled to have fun.

Life is most definitely for living, and I want to go out of this world knowing that I've squeezed every inch of enjoyment out of it and done my best. Although, let's face it, I didn't have the best start in life, I'm entitled to have a bit of fun.

Although Lee Ridley, The Lost Voice Guy, adapts to being a stand-up comedian using his communication aid very well, It's not the kind of comedy that shows my personality very well. I love making bold statements because, in many ways, our actions can be much more effective than any spoken word. Think about it: a well-written slogan or a strong-minded demonstration speaks volumes and is way more inclusive.

I've already written about how my parents wanted me to be visible and included from an early age. Our friends immediately bought into that vision, so much so that I'm there on every trip or occasion. Here in Wales, we love a good old knees-up or night out and, on many occasions, a good sing-along. We are a nation of rugby-mad nutters, too. It's in our blood, and we've become one of the most respected rugby nations worldwide.

I, now and again like an outing to watch a local game or even a trip to our national stadium, 'The Principality,' to watch Wales play. I also love attending an event where a sporting celebrity gives an after-dinner speech. I find it fascinating to hear all about what went on behind the scenes of their careers and how they cope with the pressures of being a professional sportsperson. So far, I've been to watch after-dinner events with the late Scottish rugby legend Doddie Weir, Welsh rugby legend Shane Williams, Wales national team coach Warren Gatland, the legendary Pontypool, Wales and British Lions Front Row Graham Price, Bobby Windsor, and Charlie Faulker, Jonathan 'Jiffy' Davies, who represented Wales in both rugby union and rugby league, and New Zealand back-row Zinzan Brooke.

THE WELCOME T-SHIRT JOKE

I returned to how I like to make bold and sometimes funny statements. I was around the age of twenty-one and staying on the rugby theme. Every two years, around February, we make a rugby-mad Welsh pilgrimage to Scotland to watch our two rugby teams lock horns in the prestigious Six Nations, and this particular year was my first time to Scotland for rugby. Bearing in mind that the group I went with had decided to go for a whole week instead of the obligatory weekend, like most sensible people, not us.

There were people on the trip I'd never met before, and being different, my anxiety and internal ableism again came over me. All that was going through my mind was, 'what if they won't understand me? I probably won't fit in with the rest of the group.' Therefore, I needed to do something to break the ice from the start.

So after thinking about it and being as crazy as I am, I went to a t-shirt printing shop and printed one with the words, 'there's no need to worry; I'm not disabled but just a little drunk.' I wore this T-shirt not only the morning the group of us met up to head to Scotland but on one occasion while we were there. My ice-breaking T-shirt most certainly went down a storm. For one, everyone was in stitches with laughter, and most importantly, the design did precisely what it was supposed to do: break the ice and become the catalyst for sparking up conversations with most random people. My disabilities became secondary, my personality shone through, and people came to know the real me.

THE NEVER ENDING TRAIN JOURNEY

We had so much fun in Scotland; it was one of the best trips I have been on. I sat by a Chinese lady and conversed with her on a train ride from Kilcaldy to where we stayed in Dunfermline. The problem was due to my severe speech impediment and her speaking in Chinese. We could not understand one another but only through hand gestures and botched sign language. However, we were so engaged in trying to work out where our conversation was leading that my friends and I were in floods of tears watching all this unfold. I still can't remember or have the foggiest idea what the conversation was about until this very day, and still, people talk about this day with fond laughter.

Unfortunately, we missed our stop and had to get off at the next station to return, which was quite a long way down the line. However, I can report that the train conductor found it funny too, and we only got charged to get back to Dunfermline a little later than expected, which meant we missed our hotel's evening meal.

THE DAY I ALMOST SOLD A LAND ROVER

On a day at the races when there were no seats around. My legs were in quite a bit of pain. So I noticed a salesperson sitting on a chair next to a Land Rover for which they were doing a sales pitch. I had seen the salesperson pop into the toilet, so I bagged a little 'rest-time' on his seat next to the brand new Land Rover, during which a lady started asking me questions about the Land Rover. Despite my speech impediment, she still clearly thought I was a salesman.

Luckily, the Land Rover was open, so I could show her around. I made up some of its specifications, and she was listening. But the salesperson returned from his nature trip and saw me talking to the woman, to which I got an outraged response in the heat of the moment. But a little while later, the gentleman came and found my friends, and he apologised for his anger, confirmed he had made a sale, and thanked me for my fantastic sales pitch. It's fair to say that my friends were again in tears of laughter.

I'M NOT A WIND-UP, I SWEAR!

I'm your average guy who is always on the cusp of the next big thing (maybe I will hit the 'big time' one day). I'm pretty crazy, the lovable soul of any party, and just an average, hard-working guy. But I like to become a joker more often. Am I a wind-up merchant? Yes, of course, but I know my limits and the value of respect because my parents have taught me that respect is something earned and not a given, a value I still honour today.

I'm also a forward thinker, and I always try to look for ways to make the world that we live in a more educated and inclusive one.

THE STEVEN GERRARD COMPETITION

So, back to the more wicked side of my personality and how I sometimes like winding people up, one of my best friends, Tony, is an avid Liverpool football supporter. I call it a stupid obsession, but he calls it love and passion for some ridiculous reason. I'm a football fan, too, and a Manchester United fan. I have been a United supporter all my life, and my most memorable period was the era of 'The King, Eric Cantona, and the likes of Steve Bruce, Roy Keane, and Mark Hughes. I have many memorabilia items, including many autographs and an official media team sheet from a United versus Barcelona mid-week European game at Old Trafford. So, I'm not that obsessed. Honestly!

Steven Gerrard left Liverpool a few years ago and was heading for LA Galaxy. At the time, Tony was distraught. I thought that he may have needed counselling for his separation anxiety. I tried to tell him that there's more to life than an average middle-of-the-road football team from somewhere up in the north of the United Kingdom, but he was still wallowing in the fact that Stevie Gerrard had upsticks.

So, to save Tony from going down the possible vigorous

route of counselling, I thought that, as a good friend, I needed to let him know that Stevie Gerrard was getting on with life after Liverpool. So I set about writing him a letter (from Stevie Gerrard, obviously) inviting him, as a competition winner, to go and meet and greet the legend himself out in LA. As a competent wordsmith, I wrote out a 'genuinely fake' letter setting out everything Tony needed to do to claim his prize, put it neatly into an envelope, addressed it to Tony, and got this. I even asked another friend who works up north often to post it from in and around Anfield so the postage stamp would look like it was from Liverpool. But the final twist in my little 'wind-up' was that I included in the letter that to claim his prize, Tony had to phone the 'Liverpool Supporters Hotline' to claim his prize.

Still, as you may have guessed and with my sense of humour, the number I wrote in the letter was the **'Manchester United Supporters Hotline.'** But I thought Tony needed to be more intelligent to believe this letter was genuine. Yes, you've guessed it, he fell for my little 'wind-up' and rang the phone number I included in the letter, the 'Manchester United Supporters Hotline."

Nowadays, Tony always tells me this was the most timely and costly telephone call ever. The best and last part of this wind-up is that after Tony made this phone call, he immediately turned to social media to vent his disgust and anger about being pranked, so much so that I declined to repeat his rage and words in this book. He then blamed all his friends, including me, for his costly phone call!

Furthermore, as the blaming was hurled in every man's and woman's direction, I still managed to deny it was me and kept a straight face for six months. Still, it soon became apparent that he was getting so frustrated by all the drama that I had to tell him I had pranked him all along.

To confirm that no counselling sessions were needed by Tony at any stage before, during, or after I had pranked him. We are still good friends even to this day, and well, Stevie Gerrard does not know of this prank whatsoever.

KNOCK, KNOCK, WHO'S THERE? JUST SOME RANDOMS!

I've known Ben Lewis, one of my good friends, since I started playing junior football. He's also a partygoer and often enjoys a good knees-up, like me. Many years ago, he was dating my sister, Hollie. As you've probably guessed, he was around our house quite often as he was dating my sister, so coming to our house for dinner was normal.

It was like having a brother from another mother, and probably still is as a friend. Even though he and my sister's dating never worked out in the end and they eventually decided to separate a long time ago, Ben and I are still good friends and have quite a lot of banter while we are out socialising.

Ben is that one friend who winds you up to the max but who'll always be there for you. He has several nicknames. One is ghost, because however much sun Ben gets, he never catches a suntan. He has been whiter than white all year.

His most recent nickname is 'Mouch', like the firefighter character Randall McHolland from the American drama series Chicago Fire, because Ben sometimes has one of those handlebar moustaches like Mouch. He does look like him. I won't say what he calls me because you may get offended, but over the years, I've taken being called this name on the chin because, however many times I ask him not to call me it, he does it more to annoy me.

You probably have worked out where I'm going with this, and with me being the ever-serial practical joker and since Ben decided to give me an unsavoury nickname, Ben has felt the wrath of one of my pranks in the past. I can only tolerate so much annoyance from a whiter-than-white individual in a playful manner.

This practical joke happened when Joe Calzaghe was boxing at the top of his game and fighting in America. It was a big fight for the WBO Super-Middleweight World Title. I knew Ben had invited a few close friends to his house to watch this fight. Still, little did Ben know that I already had a mischievous plan up my sleeve. I knew that he would only be staying at our local pub after he'd played football for our village team for a bit before going home in readiness to welcome people into his home. So I printed out pre-fight posters inviting everyone to Ben's house, complete with his address, to watch the fight and enjoy some light snacks. Just bring your beer. I put it this way to make it sound convincing, as you do!

When he left, I asked one of our other friends to help me put the posters on every noticeboard and wall at our local club. All I had to do then was hope that my prank would be of heavyweight proportions (see what I did there)! Would go the distance (sorry for the terrible punchline jokes!). I couldn't resist. At this point, I had a vision in my head from one of those American high school movies where, in the summer holidays, one pupil's parents go on vacation, or holiday, as we say in the UK. One of the pupil's more mischievous school friends finds out and sends a message to every pupil to turn up for a party, and it ends up in pure carnage just because this was to happen at Ben's house in Wales. Perfect!

Some people weren't regular drinkers, and visitors were drinking at our local that late afternoon into the evening, and being the enjoyable soul that I am, I introduced myself. I also pointed out the posters where most people read them, and I did notice that people were leaving my local soon after reading them. It was empty.

Cut to a few days later, during a mid-week football training session. Ben couldn't wait to tell the rest of our friends about the previous Saturday night or Sunday morning when he had random strangers knocking on his door at inappropriate hours, desperate to watch the Calzaghe fight. Little did he realise he had been caught up in one of my practical joke masterplans until the lads told him my comedic genius had caught him out, and not just some high school leavers from America like in the movies. He did really see the funny side of my action plan when he next saw me, and we are all still good friends, and he still calls me that unsavoury nickname.

NOTHING WRONG WITH A GOOD OLD PRANK!

Life is too short to be serious all the time. Sometimes, a good prank or a knockout of a practical joke (that's the last punchline for now, I promise) can become more meaningful than words, especially for someone like me with a speech impediment.

As you can see, making funny statements or becoming the joker is a trait I use to portray my personality. But, as I have already talked about, there is an element of risk that needs to be understood. Sometimes unintentionally and even, on occasion, intentionally or for other people's gain. Still, they say taking no risks will be your most significant risk, and if the most considerable risk I take is making a bold statement as a small part of my advocacy for society to become more understandably inclusive, but, then, it's a risk well worth taking.

CHAPTER 11
THE LOVER

"Being disabled should not mean being disqualified from having access to every aspect of life." —**Emma Thompson**

FINDING LOVE WITH A DISABILITY

A close second to being anxious about my speech impediment is finding love and leaping into the dating scene. It has been another tricky part of my life. Physically and emotionally, I have found it very hard. I'm now in my forties, and I need to use the process of writing this book as a realisation that when it comes to getting close to someone, yes, and falling in love, I have been and am still scared to death to do so. When I think about it and delve deep into why I haven't let someone love me, I have almost traumatised myself into thinking that I am not worthy of being loved because of my physical differences.

There have been times when I've had a slight chance of flirtatious glances and interactions from women, and I've walked away due to all my frustration and worry bubbling up inside. I often struggle to think of or even imagine myself getting close to and sexually physical with a woman. Insecurities enter my head, and I convince myself that sexually, I may never be able to satisfy her needs, which would, over time, affect the relationship. She will end up leaving anyway.

I've got to face the fact that it's my own doing, and mentally, I've built a steel fortress around me from a young age. I've yet to be able to break through it, and truthfully, I know this is the exact reason why I have struggled to fully accept myself as disabled, even though I have come a long way in my acceptance journey since writing my first children's book. I'm still not in a place where I can fully accept myself as a disabled man. I sometimes think, 'Would I now be in a relationship if I wasn't disabled?"

THERE IS SOMEONE FOR EVERYONE

My family and friends always try to tell me that all this frustration and worrying about letting my guard down is all in my head, and I need to relax and be myself, and the rest will fall into place. There's somebody out there for everyone. But, up until this point, I've failed to smash through the steel fortress surrounding my heart and find the confidence I so desperately yearn for to enable me to find love. Another fly in the ointment is that I often need a bit of courage and a few beers to have any chance of chatting someone up. Yes, as you've guessed, either my chat-up lines are terrible, or I fall asleep after a few tipples or even go into my shell again with my steel fortress rising over me. I could be the real-life Henry Roth or Adam Saddler, like in the film '50 First Dates', always overthinking and finding stupid new ways to win over the girl of my dreams.

I've gone through complex scenarios in my head and asked myself many questions, like, if I met someone, would it be like a 'carers' relationship rather than a 'lovers' one? Will she leave me if somebody more capable steals her heart? As a couple, would we become a laughingstock because of my disabilities?

Also, I know yet again I'm resorting back to hiding behind my speech impediment and the anxiety I have experienced with it. Maybe I am using the fear of not being understood when I want to chat with a lady I become attracted to as an excuse to not unlocking the fortress I have around me and consider discussing all of my fears about finding someone with a professional counsellor or therapist who could help elevate my worries surrounding my fears.

The worry of getting hurt or heartbroken also plays on my mind. I get that becoming heartbroken can happen to anyone, but along with the million and one other things, you tend to overthink and worry about many things being disabled. Not letting my heart be torn apart is something I can be in control of.

I have sometimes found it challenging to work out if a girl is genuinely attracted to me. Are they just being nice or showing me pity? I would often quietly walk off the dance floor in a strop, go to the bar for another drink, and find somewhere to sit down on my own because I get that condescending feeling draining right through me. Whenever this condescending feeling starts to kick in, I hate feeling like it.

I advise people wanting to interact with disabled people on nights out to treat them the same as anyone else. Make your intentions clear, because we tend to overthink or misjudge those signs. Our expectations for trying to nail down a relationship are very high. So if you want to dance the night away and chat, clear those attentions, or if you think genuine attraction is present, make your feelings known. Be open.

THE WHATIFS

My sister and brother are married and in long-term relationships. Admittedly, I often wonder if I will ever have my own family, and I sometimes let my anxiety kick in and let myself overthink and wonder if I will settle down. Unfortunately, I can't get past the point of thinking my disabilities are holding me back from finding someone. Maybe I should take a leaf out of Rod Stewart's or Ronnie Wood's books, embrace my inner rock god, get a skin-tight white pair of jeans, show my hairy chest, and bling myself up. It has worked for them later in life. Still, you never know what lies around any corner, and they say love can strike when you least expect it. So maybe I'll finally settle down in my, let's say, more elegant and sensible years?

Life begins at forty, they say. But in all seriousness, I often see on social media and hear others with disabilities say that the best advice they can give is that you need to learn to fall in love with yourself entirely. That's when you'll allow yourself to be loved by others. Truthfully, I am getting there. After all, this is part of why I wrote my children's book, Max and the Magic Wish, about disability and acceptance and to let disabled children know it's okay to accept others and be accepted by others. Perhaps, subconsciously, another reason I wrote my first children's book is to tell myself that it is time now to look back to when I accepted the younger version of me all those years ago, fall in love with myself entirely, and find the one. Who knows, maybe Max will grow up to find true love someday.

CHAPTER 12
THE FRIEND

"Know me for my abilities, not my disability." —**Robert M. Hensel**

As discussed earlier in this book, my family and friends have always seen, known, and treated me like anyone else. You know the saying, 'treat people how you want to be treated.' Well, I'm lucky to live by this saying.

The days when I played football and started secondary school—looking back, this was one of those turning points in life that sticks in my mind because it was when I felt I genuinely became accepted as 'one of the boys.' I made friends and became a friend to others; until this day, these friendships are still formed even though life and people have moved on to bigger and better things, moved away, or found the loves of their lives and now have their own families. I often think to myself and wonder, if I were not disabled, would I have now moved away or met my love and settled down? After all this, I am still crazy. Even in my forties, I still like to party, even though my body is starting to tell me to slow down. But we are dealt the cards we are dealt, and how I look at it, I am yet to play my queen of hearts and my ace. I'm just waiting for the perfect time to lay them down, and that's when I'll finally settle down. Or even if I don't get to play these cards. My social life has been lived to the fullest.

Growing up with the friends I have made has been unbelievable, and we've made so many memories over the years. Pentwynmawr is a great community, support-wise, to have grown up in and will continue to be one. However, even from a disability perspective, the landscape is tough to navigate. It's hilly, and these valleys are topsy-turvy, but still, I have survived playing in the heart of these villages and have come out the other end with just a few cuts, bruises, broken bones, and aching legs. Unfortunately, there may be a few more accidents with these unreliable legs of mine.

I'm so grateful that I'm not confined to a wheelchair, because I believe I wouldn't have been as socially active and made as many great friends. Still, I know I am incredibly more fortunate than others to have been able to walk, even if it's in my little, unreliable way. I will always be so grateful for the life I have been blessed with and will continue to respect other disabled people's values. I will always support them.

COMMUNITY IS EVERYTHING

Years ago, everybody knew everybody well in these parts of the world. You even called your mother's friends Aunty when they visited you or you went to their houses, and their doors were always open. You felt safe in your own homes. I often went to a friend's house after school or vice versa for food, and we'd often have sleepovers. Summer fetes and street parties would usually happen, with everyone from the village getting involved.

On one occasion, the village came together for a fundraising event to help me buy my first augmentative and alternative communication device, my Light Writer. I remember, amongst other activities, that the focal point of the fundraising effort was to bail Santa out of jail in time for Christmas. Someone from the village dressed up as Santa and was locked up in a cell at a local police station. All in good fun, and I can clarify that he got released at double-quick speed after hitting our fundraising target, and the local press interviewed him.

I have made so many friends through playing football. In those days, junior football games were played on Saturday mornings. The friends I played football with became good friends, and we'd often hang out after football and on Saturday afternoons. Especially after the games were over and we had showered and changed, we would go into the local community centre for post-match food, soup, and sweets. Then, if the senior team played at home, we'd watch their game, or if they were playing away, we'd again play a game between ourselves. We were football-mad!

In the summer and out of the football season, we would play a game of runouts in and around the village. It is a game where you pick two even sides out of how many people are present, and both teams go their separate ways, and the first team to find every player out of the opposing team wins. I used to hide somewhere where nobody could see me. But, of course, there were plenty of places to hide in people's gardens and rose bushes.

In Pentwynmawr, and for as long as I can remember, an extinct railway line ran underneath and through to the other end of the village and beyond. Not so much now because housing developments are built there, but you could hide in the tunnel, which is still there. Or there were plenty of uncanny or overgrown culverts I'd submerge myself in, and I'd usually stay there for hours, not getting caught out, or until my mother called for me to go home. It was great fun. Then, as we all grew a little older, we became a little more naughty and often played a game of knock-knock ginger. To save myself from getting caught knocking on a door because I could not run away quickly, I used to hide beside or even underneath a parked car. I would then wait until the residents of the door we knocked on answered and shut the door, or until the others were getting chased, and then run at my own pace and, in my quirky little way, in the other direction. Great times!

We also loved playing on our skateboards and lived at the top of a steep street. I couldn't stand up on a moving skateboard or a stagnant one. So, I used to position my skateboard facing down the road with a significant incline. I sat on it and used my hands to get going, and by the time I had reached the bottom, I had built up some impressive speeds. Thinking back now, though, it was dangerous because if a moving car ever turned the corner, it got scary. Either I had to manoeuvre out of the way by leaning left or right, or the car had to break. It was a high-risk game and a stupid one on my part. Still, I lived to see another day.

Later in life, as we grew into teenagers and maybe for a few years beyond, we'd still 'hang out' in and around the village as teenagers do. Then dating started—not as if I hooked up with any girls. Friday nights, we'd walk through the lanes and onto the next village, Newbridge, and meet lots of other friends at a local park called Top Park and drink alcopops, or for quite a few years, there were discos put on in the local Memorial Hall to keep us off the streets; these were great fun.

FOOTBALL TOURS

Even though I didn't progress to youth and senior football with my friends, I was still heavily involved. I watched them every Saturday if they were playing home or away, and up until a few years ago, I always attended an end-of-season tour. These days, I'm more selective about the ones I go on due to my commitments. The old saying goes, 'What happens on tour stays on tour.' Still, I'm going to tell one little story.

We had gone to Newcastle this particular year, and my

friend Ben had arranged the trip. He was so excited about being the organiser. He had bragged for months about how he'd found accessible accommodation where my father and I had a downstairs accessible twin room to enable me to get dressed and sleep easily. But when I got to the room, the best way to describe it was like being in a dungeon. The floors were uneven and creaked. Beds were propped up with house bricks, and to have a shower, you had to attach the shower head and wire from it to the hot water tap on the sink and shower as best you could. Still, with help from my father, I just about managed to dress.

It was the first day, and Ben was, let's say, excited. We had all unpacked and were ready to leave 'the dungeon' for fun and drinks. Still, we had to walk a little way to get to the town centre, and while we were walking, Ben's excitement went into overdrive, for the reason that he only knows. Ben decided to turn into James Bond and do a forward dive over what seemed like a small wall but was unknown to us. There was a considerable drop on the other side of the wall, meaning he went for much more of a dive than he anticipated. Still, Ben forgot to use his hands to protect himself, landed on his chin, and bit the end of his tongue off in the process, which at the time was horrific. He ended up in the hospital for surgery, and his father drove to Newcastle to take him home days later. So, for one, the moral of this story is always to check the other side of any wall before excitedly jumping over it, and secondly, moments like these stay with you forever.

My friends have stuck by me through my dark times and

good times, and I thank everyone who has accepted me as I am. Even these days, it's occasions like these that we still talk and laugh about, and that's what good friends are for. They stick by you and make memories you'll discuss when you grow old together.

I have highlighted numerous times in this book that my parents weren't afraid of letting me find my own way in life, and up until now, it has proved to be the best decision they could have made because my life has been 'bloody great'. There have been many barriers I have had to smash through, and undoubtedly, I will stubbornly continue to smash through a few, if not for my own sake but to help create more of an inclusive and accessible society for future generations of disabled people. I want to do this and be one of many successful disabled superstars showing the way and defying many ableist characteristics we face daily.

A WALK DOWN MEMORY LANE

So, I now want to look back and take you down memory lane. I have asked a few long-time friends and colleagues who have known me for a long time to talk about our friendships and professional relationships and how we've faced many barriers, found ways to sometimes go around them, and even overcome them. I hope you enjoy this trip down my memory lane.

MY LIFELONG FRIEND, KATE!

"Gavin and I never met or were never introduced. We were both born into an extended family. Our parents were old friends; his father was the best man for my dad. In our "world", nothing was different. Gavin was Gavin. Gavin wore different shoes and a special helmet, and conversations took a lot longer, but we all had quite a normal childhood. We loved playing in the street, hide and seek in the rose gardens, "knock knock", and football! We made exceptions to allow Gavin to join in. For example, if Gavin hadn't had a head start, we would have been caught more by Mr. Matthews when playing "knock knock".

Gavin and I attended Pentwynmawr Primary School, and it was a school that indeed prided itself on inclusion. There were children with many disabilities, illnesses, and visual and hearing impairments. Gavin had a learning support assistant attached to him, so when challenges were met, he was supported. He did everything that all the other children did, and he always had a big smile. My favourite memories were all our family gatherings. We would have amazing parties and camping trips. From my understanding, Gavin's parents wanted his life to be like every other child's.

When Gavin was due to start high school, there was tremendous community support to get him a computer that would help him achieve his potential and easily transition to a new school. I remember being told Santa was locked up until enough money was raised for Gavin's computer. It was amazing how everyone came together, and this has pushed Gavin; he knows how supported he is, and so many people care for and love him.

At times, it was easy to forget that Gavin had cerebral palsy until people who didn't know Gavin entered "our world". My earliest memory of being hurt for Gavin was when a few of us were playing football together. I always hung out with the boys; for some girls, that was strange, and they wanted to make a big deal of it. We were approached by some ignorant girls who started laughing at us, and I remember Gavin telling them to "do one"; unfortunately, he was subjected to abuse and called a "cripple". This comment hurt me equally as much because Gavin was a friend, not defined by a disability, and I was certainly not used to hearing that word. This, fortunately, was a rare occasion, but one that will stick with me. Gavin had enough friends that he was usually protected from this behaviour. Sadly, this wasn't the last time I experienced such ignorance.

I, Gavin, and Adam were great friends and, as teenagers, did a lot together. One of our shared interests was the Pentwynmawr Workingmen's Club. Adam and I were only 16 and worked behind the bar, and Gavin was 18, and he liked Worthington beer. We would serve the drinks, and he would drink them. On Saturday afternoon, Gavin had gone to watch the local football team and returned to the club where me and Adam were working; well, I was working, and the two boys were playing pool. The away football team came in and was keen to play pool.

A few of the younger boys came and put their coins down on the table, spotted Adam and Gavin, and, without intention, became very patronising. I remember hearing, "Oh, look. He can even hold the pool cue!" A few wanted to shake Gavin's hand. Gavin did precisely what he should have done and handled it brilliantly. He politely insulted the boys. Adam and I had years of practice understanding Gavin despite his cleft lip, and cleft palate, but the football boys had no idea! They were laughing, smiling, and nodding, with no clue what Gavin was saying about them. He had the last laugh!

I've loved growing up with Gavin. We've shared many special times, including some great moments on the karaoke. Our friendship as adults has and will always continue. Gavin has worked hard to achieve everything he has today. We have been such a close community and supported each other as equals, and as a friend, I am incredibly proud of him. He meets all challenges with a smile, a wicked sense of humour, and the desire to do well—a lesson to us all."

Kate Storey – Gavin's Lifelong Friend

WORKING WITH GAVIN AT THE ARGUS

It's easy to avoid someone with a disability. I've seen it many times in my lifetime. You can see the awkwardness in some individuals' manners and the lengths they go to avoid contact. I'm so glad that I'm not that sort of person.

I first met Gavin in 2006, when I returned to work for the

South Wales Argus newspaper. Before I ever adequately met Gavin, I admired him from afar, and often, I would see him drive to work, park his car, and walk into the offices all by himself. I sensed it was difficult for Gavin, but he was always cheery and greeted people on the way to work. It began for me when we arrived together one day. He got to the front door before me, and through all his difficulties, he was the one who held the door for me. I thanked him and just about understood his reply. He said,

"That's alright; have a nice day." I'll never forget that gesture.

A few days later, I found myself having to speak to someone in the same department where Gavin worked. He looked up as I passed his desk and said, "Alright?" I replied, "Yes, I'm fine, and you?" He said, "Yeah, I'm alright." I carried on past him. When I returned, I noticed him tapping away on his keyboard, entering data to go into the magazine. It impressed me, and a few weeks passed.

Now and again, we would say hi or wave an acknowledgement. I remember the day he saw me coming as I passed his desk and beckoned me over. (I felt a little uneasy as Gavin's speech wasn't the best; he had heard that I was a singer and wanted to know if I knew anyone with a recording studio.) I felt a bit nervous as he was talking to me. I couldn't understand him, and although embarrassed, I said I was unsure what you were trying to say. As quick as a flash, he pointed at his screen and began to type what he was trying to tell me. Wow, was I impressed!

That's when our conversations took off. As the weeks passed, I began to understand Gavin's speech better. Still, sometimes, if Gavin was tired or excited about something, then his speech would get harder to understand, so I would say to him, Slow down, Gav. I'd give him a pen and grab a piece of paper; he would start to write, and I would then pick up the gist of the conversation. And that's how we still communicate to this day.

I love how Gavin has evolved through the years I've known him. I was so sorry to hear the news that, along with myself, he had been made redundant from his job. For a few years, we kept in touch through Facebook. Still, in the past few months, I've been able to help him with his networking, introducing him to lots of different people who, in turn, have come to see how talented this individual is and the impact he is starting to make on society, educating children and adults through the power of two published books about people with disabilities. It's incredible work, and that's just the tip of the iceberg with all the fundraising he has done for various groups that needed help.

Gavin, I wish you every success in taking your life experiences and telling them to the world! I know this will help lots of non-disabled people and disabled children and adults overcome the situations we all face in life. You have impacted my life, and I thank you for it. Good luck with everything you do.

Pam Appleby, Director at Go Local Magazine and Print Limited and Gavin's friend.

BEING GAVIN'S BOSS

I'm Lynda, or "Boss" to Gavin. That's what Gav officially called me for over ten years and still does to this day. I was his line manager when he worked at the South Wales Argus newspaper. And when I say worked, well, most days a week, I got him working. Some days, well, Gav is Gav. When necessary, I would crack the whip, but occasionally he would brush me off and flash a smile. He could get away with murder that boy. He's a charmer.

From what we can both remember, Gavin was employed as a typist by Roy Kerr, whom Gavin thought was a bit mad. As the business expanded into supplements for the newspapers, Gavin believes he blagged his way into the desktop publishing department. Anyway, so Gavin ended up on my small team. We created all the newspaper supplements that sold houses way before everything like this got sold online. The job was relentless and complicated, using desktop publishing software and databases. It was always stressful at the last minute, and the hours were long. A couple of nights a week, on press deadlines, it wasn't unusual to be there until after midnight. Gav would be there, digging in with the rest of the team to get the paper completed—a real team player.

If you know Gav, you can see his disability. It limits his mobility and coordination. Having to use a mouse and keyboard was a major problem. It looks difficult for him, favouring his better hand, but it never showed in his quality or throughput. With his immense determination to be as good, if not better than others doing the same job, Gavin was a great asset to the team.

Liaising with the customers and the rest of the team could often be challenging and hilarious. Within weeks of spending every day with Gavin, my understanding of his speech became very good, and this was only sometimes the case with others. Gav would never get frustrated but would throw in the odd swear word at the bosses who couldn't understand him and get me to be his early version of his speech app. It was always a pleasure. Gav is always good fun on a night out. As I said, he's a charmer. He's funny as hell, and when in Pentwynmawr, he's a minor celebrity.

As for his driving, well, let's say it's an experience. Gav once picked me and my husband up for a night out in the 'Mawr''. When he arrived at the pick-up point, he got out of the car, and it was my husband's first time meeting Mr. Clifton. I could see on his face that he was wondering if getting in the car was a good idea. As I said previously, Gav will have his own way of doing things to make the most of his condition. With his adapted car and his supreme confidence in himself, let's say Gav drives a car like he's stolen it. On getting to the pub, my husband was white as a sheet and vowed never to get in the car with Gav again.

Since we both left The Argus, we have kept in touch. And then, through COVID, the world changed. Gav became super creative, and we all took time to see how we could contribute to the world. Gav's Max book came out; I bought one, and my husband read it. He was emotional and wanted to do something. Fortunately, the stars aligned, and through the lockdown, he had been bringing authors and books to thousands of kids in Wales via live online lessons through his employer, the Stephens and George Charitable Trust. The previous week, they had the fortune to have BBC newsreader Lucy Owen read her new children's novel to 2000 children. Lucy is the patron of a cerebral palsy charity. What a result! Weeks later, Gav had his life story video short created on the internet, financed by the trust. This led to Lucy getting his story on the BBC Wales teatime news. A star was born. And it was bloody fantastic that the world (well, those in Wales) also got to meet my friend.

I adore the gentleman; he is a credit to his lovely family. I love you, Gav.

Lynda Donovan, Property Supervisor at The South Wales Argus

CHAPTER 13
THE FUTURE

"I don't know what lies around the bend, but I'm going to believe that the best does." —**L. M. Montgomery**

It's fair to say that from day one of my life, The odds weren't entirely in my favour. Even today, I can do the things I have been able to do, even though I have had to sometimes improvise how I do something to enable me to live my life the best I can, especially when I decided to enter this world arse-backwards, not breathing, and immediately dicing with death before even getting to meet my parents. Still, I have made it to tell the tale, or more to the point, to write this book.

WHERE AM I RIGHT NOW?

Life throws us all challenges, whether we are disabled or not. We aim to savour the good times, endure them, and try to work through the bad ones. We wouldn't be humans if we never went through the rollercoaster of living life, sometimes on the edge. But you could argue that people with disabilities are thrown different challenges throughout their lives than most, not always by their own doing but because of the daily barriers they face like accessibility in physical environments and on the internet, social exclusion, the lack of assistive technology, and barriers in healthcare and the workplace.

As you've read in this book, I have faced some of these barriers head-on. I've tackled a few head-on with some degree of success, and with others, I've had to swallow my stubborn pride and concede that I'll never be able to change or move.

Writing this book has been a rollercoaster, and it has made me realise that even though I consciously believe I have made steps towards self-acceptance, there are still areas of my life and even my way of thinking that I still need to work on discovering and making better so I can get to a place where I can be truly happy as a disabled man.

Although I will always be Gavin Clifton, The Disabled Writer, with cerebral palsy and a speech impediment, it has been sometimes challenging throughout my life. As we all grow through life, we change as people. Occasionally, we get stronger, and sometimes we crumble. But I am a very strong-minded and proud person. I inherited this from my dad's mother, my grandmother Maggie, who many people have said was one of the most determined women they'd ever known.

WHAT THE FUTURE HOLDS

I believe emotionally and deeply that, throughout my life, I have changed from being a little more carefree twenty years ago to being a little more aware and apprehensive about my differences than I was earlier in life. I am delving deeper into why and thinking about why; maybe I'm worrying too much about getting old and having disabilities. We all get old and sometimes become less mobile. That's a given, but the uncertainty of not knowing when my body's condition could get worse and worse, possibly disconnecting me from my social activities, friends, and maybe my writing, which I love the most right now, I'm perhaps missing and yearning for my younger self, my younger body, and again, overthinking myself to possibly get disconnected from the things and people I value the most.

SO, WHAT'S IN STORE FOR THE FUTURE?

I think I've used the beginning of this chapter to establish my concerns about getting old with a disability. I want to use the achievement of finishing and publishing my autobiography as a wake-up call and reminder that I am only bloody human, just like everyone else, and whenever I fall back into 'overthinking mode', remember to instantly remind myself how lucky I am to have done and achieved the things I have. Not everyone gets the opportunities and support I have been so fortunate to have, whatever their situation or abilities.

I am very hard on myself, and instead of waiting for things that are maybe out of my reach or out of my control, It's time I try to manage my expectations and take life as it comes because I'm not getting any younger and I can't rewrite the past or change who I am. With every milestone I make and everything I do, my ambitions and expectations are sky-high, and I may need to get into the mindset of lowering them. Not too much, though.

It's time to, from here on in, search for and unleash that little carefree boy I was back in the Max and the Magic Wish story on a journey bossing his way to becoming fully accepted and accepting of others and begin enjoying life whilst never giving up on it and being the person that inspires and shines a beacon of hope for others. I wrote this book to make a difference and educate others about what you can achieve despite being different. I need to stop worrying about factors I cannot control, concentrate on myself wholesomely, and own the carefree and always-be-you spirit that I so much have in abundance deep down, not forgetting to be the same old funny and wind-up merchant person I have always been all my life while opening myself up to working towards letting myself be loved by someone as a partner, embracing all the fun and happy adventures this person could end up opening in my life.

As I have written right at the beginning of this book, we are all entitled to our opinions on how we want to live our lives, and we only learn and adjust our paths by making our own mistakes and judgements. We are all entitled to our own opinions and choices, and with every choice I have made thus far, whether bad or good, I have done so with the intent to learn from whatever actions or consequences come from those actions and intentions and keep on navigating life's journey the best I can. It's fair to say that there will always be someone who disagrees with how I live with disabilities, whether I make the right or wrong choices.

Throughout my life, I have been very fortunate to have many people who love and support me. I admit, because of my stubborn and independent streak, I don't thank and tell everyone how much I love them, value them, and am so thankful to have them as often as I should. I owe them so much because every step of the way, these people have stood by me, accepted me as I am, and fought with me and my family to break down so many barriers so I could live the life that I am now.

MAKING THE WORLD A BETTER PLACE

I would love to use my story, experiences, and visible presence to improve everything, making the world a more accessible and inclusive place for people with all disabilities. That would be amazing. But the truth is, nobody, even up until this day, has been able to do this, and I am sure no one alone will ever be able to become the trigger or key that unlocks every inaccessible barrier. We all, as a society, need to find a way to banish past judgmental stereotypes and focus on opening as many doors and opportunities as we can to make disability awareness a key focal point and talking point within the areas of society willing to educate themselves that every disabled person has a value and right to become a vital part of everyday life, even though we may look or act differently from the societal norm. Even if, in my lifetime, we see an upturn in disability awareness being seriously discussed in our schools and educational system, with these discussions acknowledged by the authorities, In my eyes, things would be moving in the right direction.

I'm so fortunate to have had the chance to have a mainstream education, play junior football as a disabled person, find employment and hold down a job for seventeen years, become a songwriter and enjoy music, and then be lucky enough to meet Clare, who has supported me so much every step of the way on my author's journey.

Due to the barriers many disabled people face daily, it's such a challenge even today, with medical advancements and modern technology, for disabled people to be heard, work, follow their dreams, and become acknowledged for what they can do as opposed to what they can't do. I still am, even today, bumping into so many societal barriers that stop me in my tracks. Still, here's the thing: this stubborn, never-give-up mindset I've had to nurture from day one is still running through my veins. It will never leave me until the day I die. Suppose I can use this crazy journey to be another voice and a piece of the disability community striving to advocate for a more inclusive, accessible, and understanding society. In that case, it will all have been worth it.

CHAPTER 14
HOPE

"Start by doing what's necessary; then do what's possible; and suddenly you are doing the impossible." -**Francis of Assisi**

It's time to combine the power of specialist technologies like augmented and alternative communication, artificial intelligence, and virtual reality to help us educate the world on inclusiveness.

I hope you're still reading this book and I haven't bored you into a state of hypnosis to the point where you have already decided to use this book to prop up that broken table leg. For this last chapter, we have done something different. I have yet to temporarily turn into a future-hopping movie star who features in movies time-travelling into the future—not quite yet, anyway. But I want to finish this book, leaving you all with a sense of hope and now wanting to learn more about all kinds of disability awareness so you can become aware of how to become a more inclusive ally for disabled people.

I have asked Clary Saddler, who I sometimes work with creatively, to discuss her area of expertise in inclusive arts and how she uses new assistive technologies, AI and AAC to improve accessibility. You may find some of this chapter helpful; conversely, it could even send you into a frenzy of confusion. However, just read on and nod your head, pretending you understand everything, because there's one thing I'm sure of: technologies like these will only continue to make life for the disabled community easier, more accessible, and more inclusive.

Nobody knows what the future holds for us all, and if they did, would that make them immortal? I always look forward to ways to improve our lives, especially for disabled people who may face different daily challenges from others. Aside from finding ways to make our everyday chores more efficient, I am a tech nerd. The joy I feel when I discover a new gadget that can make my life easier as a disabled man is overwhelming. I'm as hyperactive as a child on Christmas morning who ate a giant tube of Smarties, if you didn't know better. I secretly have this feeling because AAC and artificial intelligence have started to creep into society and even more so into my life.

MY LOVE-HATE RELATIONSHIP WITH AAC

After my love-hate relationship with AAC throughout school and now rediscovering my genuine need and love for it not long ago, my life has improved and will continue to do so because of improving disability aids and new technology evolving constantly.

There are many companies and organisations out there now that are making strides and breaking down barriers. For example, I work with Clary Saddler, the co-founder and artistic director of Forget-Me-Not Productions, who specialises in working with people with complex physical and cognitive disabilities.

Alongside her wife, Mel, Forget-Me-Not Productions uses assistive technologies to make the arts (music, drama, film, and visual arts) accessible to everyone. Just as I do, Clary and Mel also believe in the essential and core values of using assistive technologies in our daily lives, which plays a massive role in why we work so well together. People with various disabilities are beginning to be empowered more, more included in all aspects of society, and more readily exploring ways to become more independent. They are beginning to educate people with a message: whatever our abilities are, nothing stops us from getting involved and being included. Still, much more could be done in the mainstream, including on our TV screens and social media, to show this.

I asked Clary to tell me how assistive technology makes the

everyday lives of disabled people more accessible and to explain in a little more detail how this technology intertwines and assists people with all kinds of disabilities.

CLARY SADDLER—FORGET-ME-NOT-PRODUCTIONS

"Forget-Me-Not-Productions has worked with some truly inspirational disabled individuals—Gavin included—who flourish within the creative arts despite the barriers they may face. Forget-Me-Not Productions can plan activities and experiences that meet the needs of everyone. Our clients include those cognitively functioning at a cause-and-effect level, so we use music and the arts at a more therapeutic level.

We also regularly work with individuals with complex physical disabilities who have typical cognitive functioning. When activities are arranged in such a way, all can become active participants in the arts using assistive technology instead of music or art therapy, (which focuses on the therapeutic aspects without always encouraging independent participation).

When doing assistive technology assessments to try and find the most appropriate access methods, for example, eyegaze, switches, direct access (touch or using a mouse alternative such as a rollerball), or low-tech AAC (such as eye pointing), we have found that music is an excellent motivator to engage individuals in assistive technology activities. This inspired us to develop a framework called Music-Can.

. . .

Each **MUSIC-CAN** session is tailored to the individual. We always assume competence and have a positive 'can-do' attitude throughout the sessions. We believe in active observation of those responses to evaluate and assess them. The subtlest and tiniest change in movement or facial expression is a powerful communicative response."

MUSIC-CAN level 1:

"These sessions are for individuals at the pre-cause and effect or cause and effect level. They will also explore the concept of choice-making. There will be no right or wrong option. The focus will be on developing very early communications. Running parallel to this will allow the assistive technology specialist to assess the most appropriate technology access method."

MUSIC-CAN level 2:

"This session is for individuals who have learned more deliberate choice-making. It enables them to put their skills into action. It also provides them with an introduction to functional communication. They will use an appropriate device to choose, direct, and comment on the activities (change instruments, sing more of one song, be quieter or louder, etc.). There are greater opportunities to work cooperatively and gain greater awareness of others. It is also an opportunity to work on the consolidation of early skills."

MUSIC-CAN level 3:

"This session level assumes that the individual is competent in using their assistive technology. It also assumes they will need assistive technology programmed appropriately to enable them to access specialist or mainstream software. The individual described in the Level 3 Case Study has been working with the Forget-Me-Not team for seven years to get to this level. Although he was a cognitively able man, his motivation and self-esteem were low when we began working with him. We have worked through many developmental stages to reach this point. He is now an up-and-coming songwriter and filmmaker. His music video was featured at Raw Ffest 2019. He was also interviewed for this by BBC Radio Wales' morning and evening show, 'Good Morning/Evening Wales'. In addition to this, an article on him was featured in Classic FM online."

https://youtu.be/pMASjievnsA

Further, I asked Clary about how assistive technology makes the lives of disabled people more accessible. I emailed her some quick-fire questions about her future hopes, how she thinks artificial intelligence will feature, and how she believes we can educate and become more visible as a disabled community. These are her thoughts:

. . .

Future hopes and aspirations regarding combining music and traditional songwriting methods with specialist technology:

"My future hopes and aspirations are centred around showcasing the power of collaboration between disabled and non-disabled songwriters and music makers. I aim to demonstrate that by combining traditional songwriting methods with specialist technology, we can continue to break down barriers and create inclusive opportunities. I want to highlight the immense talent and creativity within the disabled community and emphasise that disability does not hinder artistic expression or the ability to contribute meaningfully. I want to see schools and educational establishments embrace the various software and assistive technology packages, so, I no longer hear individuals with physical or cognitive disabilities saying that music-making and/or songwriting is not for them."

The role of AI in contributing to this:

"AI can play a significant role in enhancing accessibility and inclusivity. AI can contribute by developing advanced assistive technologies that enable individuals with disabilities to fully participate in songwriting and music-making activities. For example, AI-powered music composition tools can assist in generating melodies, chord progressions, and harmonies, providing a foundation for collaboration. AI can also aid in automating certain aspects of the production process, making it more accessible for individuals with physical disabilities. By leveraging AI, we can create tools and platforms that empower disabled songwriters and amplify their voices."

When incorporating AI-generated voices or voice emulators for singing purposes to aid non-verbal creators, several factors should be considered:

Generating Melodies and Pitch:

"AI can create melodies and pitch sequences using input parameters or patterns provided by non-verbal creators by inputting musical notation or specifying melodic patterns. AI models can generate synthesised voices that correspond to the desired output. This empowers non-verbal individuals to explore and create melodies without relying on traditional singing skills."

Synthesising Vocal Expressions:

"AI-powered vocal synthesis techniques can produce singing voices that mimic human vocal characteristics. By training on a vast dataset of singing samples, AI models can generate expressive and realistic singing voices. Non-verbal creators can input lyrics and melodies, and the AI-generated voice can sing the desired composition.

Modifying Voices: AI enables the transformation of existing voices to match different singing styles or genres. Through adjustments to vocal attributes like timbre, pitch, vibrato, or intonation, non-verbal creators can modify their voices using AI and achieve the desired singing style."

Collaboration with Vocalists:

"Non-verbal creators can collaborate with human vocalists (like I do with Gavin and Mr X as part of our songwriting initiative, Word Groove Collective) and utilise AI as a tool to enrich their collaborative music-making process. AI-generated voices can blend with human vocals, resulting in unique and collaborative performances. This allows non-verbal creators to contribute to music creation while collaborating with skilled vocalists.

It is essential to acknowledge that while AI-generated singing voices can be beneficial for non-verbal creators, they may not fully capture the subtleties and expressiveness of a human voice. Nevertheless, ongoing advancements in AI technology continue to improve the quality and realism of AI-generated singing voices.

Using AI-generated singing voices as a tool in music production provides fresh opportunities for self-expression and artistic exploration. It enables individuals to engage in music creation and share their musical ideas with the world, even in the absence of traditional singing abilities."

HERE ARE SOME POPULAR AI-POWERED SINGING VOICE EMULATORS AND CREATORS YOU CAN CONSIDER:

Jukedeck by OpenAI: Jukedeck is an AI music composition tool that enables users to generate custom music tracks, including vocal melodies and harmonies. While it doesn't offer individual singing voices, it provides a comprehensive music creation experience.

VOCALOID by Voctro Labs: VOCALOID is a renowned software synthesiser that utilises AI technology to create singing voices. It offers a variety of virtual singers with different vocal characteristics and language options. Notable voicebanks include Hatsune Miku, Megurine Luka, and Kagamine Rin/Len.

SynthV: SynthV is another well-liked singing synthesiser that leverages AI techniques for vocal generation. It provides a diverse range of virtual singers and supports multiple languages. Popular voicebanks in SynthV include Eleanor Forte and Genbu.

CeVIO: CeVIO is a software suite encompassing speech and singing synthesis capabilities. It features AI-powered singing voices and offers customisation options to create unique vocal performances.

UTAU: UTAU is a free and open-source singing synthesiser software that empowers users to create their own singing voices, known as "UTAUloids." Although it requires manual voicebank creation, UTAU has a vibrant community of user-generated voicebanks and resources.

"It's important to note that an AI voice generator can assist in modifying a voice to sound like Sam Smith, for example. It may only partially replicate all the nuances and qualities of their voice. The outcome will depend on the capabilities of the specific AI system and the skill with which you apply the modifications. It's always advisable to approach the process with realistic expectations and understand that achieving a replica of another singer's voice may be challenging."

Educating about disabled and non-disabled collaborations:

"Collaborations involving disabled and non-disabled individuals must raise awareness and foster inclusivity."

The following initiatives and strategies can be implemented:

"Advocacy and Representation: Promote the Visibility and Representation of Disabled Songwriters and Artists Highlight success stories and showcase the valuable contributions of disabled creators through various media outlets, conferences, and industry events."

Collaborative Workshops and Training:

"Organise workshops and training sessions that bring together disabled and non-disabled songwriters, encouraging collaboration and sharing experiences. Such sessions can facilitate mutual understanding, break stereotypes, and foster relationships that lead to meaningful partnerships."

Accessibility Guidelines:

"Develop comprehensive accessibility guidelines for music production, distribution, and performance. These guidelines should address physical accessibility, the integration of assistive technology, captioning, audio description, and other relevant aspects. Encouraging music professionals to adhere to these guidelines will promote inclusivity.

Shedding light on other aspects related to this subject, it is important to address the societal perception of disability and challenge stigmas. We can pave the way for broader social change and establish a fairer society. It is crucial to acknowledge that disabled individuals possess unique perspectives and talents that can enhance the artistic landscape. Embracing diversity and inclusivity creates an environment where creativity can thrive and barriers can be overcome.

Together, through collaboration, advocacy, and the transformative power of music, we can demonstrate that differences are to be celebrated and overcome. By combining traditional songwriting methods with specialised technology and harnessing the potential of artificial intelligence, we can build a music society that authentically represents the diversity of the human experience.

Apart from specialist technologies like augmented and alternative communication and artificial intelligence, there are other ways in which technology is making the lives of disabled people more accessible and manageable. Smart home technology is helping to control our home's lighting, heating, doors, windows, kitchen utilities, and entertainment systems, all at the click of a button or the use of a mobile phone app, laptop, or tablet. There are also voice-activated hubs like Apple HomeKit, Amazon Echo (even though mine doesn't respond to me because of my naughty speech), and Google Nest."

FINAL THOUGHTS

Above are just some examples of how technology is making the lives of disabled people more manageable, accessible, diverse, and inclusive. Still, we must remember that technology changes constantly. Not every bit of technology will suit everyone; different technologies may suit people differently, maybe not even at all. As technology advances, we must be more patient and open to accepting that some people may have differences and that new technology may be around the corner that opens their eyes to a whole new world, even if it means them going about their daily lives using a computer that's replacing the norm. By accepting this and supporting them, you are then including them in society.

ALSO BY GAVIN CLIFTON

Max and the Magic Wish

Paddy the polar bear Teddy

Printed in Great Britain
by Amazon